Why You Aren't Making Money with Network Marketing

(And How to Turn It Around)

Written by

Maxwell Bridge

Indipendently published

2023

Introduction

A Glimpse into the World of Network Marketing

At first glance, network **marketing**—a business model predicated upon individual entrepreneurship and personal networks—may seem like a straightforward path to financial independence. It promises an opportunity to meld personal passions with earning potential, building a career outside the confinements of the 9-to-5 grind. However, the simplicity of this description belies the complexity and nuance inherent within the industry. It's essential to probe beneath the surface to truly grasp the multifaceted nature of network marketing.

To the uninitiated, network marketing is sometimes equated with 'pyramid schemes' or viewed with a degree of skepticism. However, such associations are the result of misconceptions rather than an accurate representation of the industry. True network marketing operates on the principles of leveraging personal relationships to sell products or services, and importantly, it offers genuine value to its customers. At its core, it's about people—connecting with them, understanding their needs, and delivering solutions that enrich their lives.

Historically, this business model has been around for over a century. Since its inception, network marketing has been an avenue for countless individuals to achieve financial freedom and personal growth. While some have garnered significant success, many others have grappled with challenges that hindered their progress.

The Essence of Network Marketing

At its most basic level, network marketing can be thought of as a blend of **direct selling** and **network building**. Independent representatives (often referred to as 'distributors' or 'associates') sell products or services directly to consumers, bypassing traditional retail spaces. These representatives earn not only from their sales but also from the sales made by the individuals they recruit into the business—forming their 'network.'

This multi-tiered earning system underscores the importance of relationship-building within the industry. Success in network marketing, contrary to some misconceptions, is not just about recruiting an endless stream of new members but ensuring that these members are well-supported, trained, and equipped to thrive. The most successful network marketers understand that their success is inextricably linked to the success of their network.

The Digital Evolution

In the era of digital transformation, network marketing has evolved considerably. Gone are the days when representatives relied solely on face-to-face interactions at home parties or local events. Today's network marketer harnesses the power of social media, e-commerce platforms, and digital marketing strategies to reach a global audience. This digital shift has democratized access, allowing even those with modest starting resources to tap into vast markets.

However, with these opportunities come challenges. The digital landscape is saturated, and standing out requires a strategic blend of authenticity, skill, and innovation. It's no longer enough to have a quality product; network marketers must craft compelling narratives, engage meaningfully with their online communities, and continuously adapt to the ever-evolving digital trends.

The Ethos of Genuine Value

It's worth emphasizing that at the heart of authentic network marketing lies a commitment to **genuine value**. Products or services pitched must stand on their own merits. This means that successful network marketers believe in what they're selling, understanding its benefits and potential impact on the customer. It's this belief, combined with business acumen, that distinguishes truly successful practitioners from those who struggle.

In conclusion, network marketing is not merely a business model—it's a dynamic ecosystem, rich in potential but also fraught with challenges. It calls for a blend of interpersonal skills, business savvy, and adaptability. As we delve deeper into the subsequent chapters, we'll unpack the intricacies of this world further, offering insights, strategies, and tools to navigate it with confidence and achieve the success you seek.

The Roadblocks You Might Face

In any journey toward success, understanding potential pitfalls is as crucial as recognizing the opportunities. With the ever-evolving landscape of network marketing, there exists a myriad of challenges, often emerging as roadblocks for both novices and seasoned professionals alike. While every individual's experience will undeniably differ, there are common challenges that permeate the industry. By understanding these roadblocks, we can better equip ourselves to navigate them, turning obstacles into opportunities.

1. Unrealistic Expectations

One of the most prevalent roadblocks is harboring unrealistic expectations. The allure of quick riches and overnight success stories can paint a skewed picture of the industry's reality. But just as Rome wasn't built in a day, true success in network marketing necessitates patience, consistent effort, and a long-term vision. *Setting unattainable short-term goals* can lead to premature disappointment and discourage further endeavors.

2. The Overwhelm of Choice

With a vast array of products, services, and companies to represent, choosing the right fit can be a daunting task. This paralysis by analysis can stall one's journey even before it truly begins. It's paramount to align with a product or service that resonates with one's personal values and market demand, ensuring genuine advocacy.

3. Inadequate Training & Mentorship

Mentorship and training serve as the bedrock for any budding network marketer. Entering the fray without proper guidance or with mentors who prioritize their own gains over genuine mentorship can lead to early disillusionment. The absence of **holistic training** that encompasses product knowledge, sales techniques, and relationship-building strategies can hamper growth.

4. The Stigma Surrounding the Industry

As previously touched upon, network marketing is sometimes marred by negative perceptions, often fueled by misconceptions and past scams.

Overcoming this ingrained stigma requires tactful communication, authenticity, and consistent evidence of value delivery.

5. Navigating the Digital Labyrinth

In today's digital age, online platforms offer tremendous outreach potential. Yet, the vastness of these platforms can be a double-edged sword. Without a well-defined digital strategy, one can easily get lost in the vastness of the internet, resulting in wasted efforts and resources.

6. Balancing Act: Personal & Professional

Blending personal relationships with business can be tricky. There's a fine line between sharing an opportunity and appearing overly aggressive or salesy. Maintaining this balance, ensuring relationships aren't strained while simultaneously growing the business, is an art that requires finesse.

7. Evolving Market Dynamics

The marketplace is not static. Trends change, consumer behaviors evolve, and staying attuned to these shifts is non-negotiable. Relying on outdated strategies or failing to adapt can render even the most seasoned marketer obsolete.

8. Financial Mismanagement

While network marketing requires minimal upfront investment compared to traditional businesses, mismanaging finances—be it overstocking on products, overspending on promotional tools, or not planning for lean periods—can lead to unnecessary financial strain.

9. Isolation and Burnout

Operating predominantly from home or outside traditional office spaces can, at times, lead to feelings of isolation. Additionally, without setting boundaries, the line between work and leisure blurs, leading to potential burnout. It's essential to cultivate a support system and set clear work-life boundaries.

Conclusion

In the words of Franklin D. Roosevelt, "A smooth sea never made a skilled sailor." The roadblocks highlighted herein, though daunting, are not insurmountable. Each challenge presents a learning opportunity, a chance to hone one's skills, and further cement their place in the vast world of network marketing. As we delve deeper into subsequent chapters, we will unpack strategies, insights, and tools to not only navigate these roadblocks but to use them as stepping stones towards unparalleled success.

Chapter 1
The Network Marketing Landscape

Historical Background

To navigate the intricate labyrinth of network marketing successfully, a comprehensive understanding of its roots and historical trajectory is paramount. Through understanding where it began, we can gain invaluable insights into its present form and likely future paths. After all, as the philosopher George Santayana wisely posited, "Those who cannot remember the past are condemned to repeat it."

1. The Birth of a New Distribution Model

Network marketing, at its core, has always been about *direct selling*. The roots of this model can be traced back to the late 19th and early 20th centuries. Avon, often regarded as the pioneer in this realm, commenced its operations in 1886. Instead of traditional retail outlets, sales were made through house-to-house visits by "Avon ladies."

2. The Conceptualization of the Network

While direct selling set the stage, the true innovation was in recognizing that every customer could also become a potential seller. By the mid-20th century, companies like Amway (founded in 1959) began leveraging this strategy. They introduced the **multi-level marketing (MLM)** structure, where individuals would not only earn from their sales but also from those made by individuals they recruited.

Tab. 1: Key Milestones in Network Marketing

Year	Event	Significance
1886	Establishment of Avon	Pioneered direct-to-consumer selling
1959	Founding of Amway	Introduced multi-level marketing
1979	Amway vs. FTC	Clarified the legal standing of MLMs
1990s	Integration of Technology	Digital platforms transform outreach

3. The Crucial Distinction: Legitimate Business vs. Pyramid Scheme

The 1970s witnessed increased scrutiny, as the blurred lines between legitimate MLM businesses and pyramid schemes became a matter of concern. The landmark case, *Amway vs. Federal Trade Commission (FTC)* in 1979, played a pivotal role in drawing a clear distinction. The FTC ruled in favor of Amway, setting forth certain guidelines differentiating legitimate MLMs from pyramid

11

schemes. At the heart of this differentiation was the stipulation that profits must primarily be derived from the sale of goods and services, rather than recruitment alone.

4. Evolution in the Age of Technology

The dawn of the internet era in the 1990s and the subsequent explosion of social media platforms in the 2000s reinvented the network marketing landscape. It magnified the outreach potential exponentially. However, with great power came great responsibility. The digital age necessitated transparency, authenticity, and adaptability more than ever before.

5. Recent Shifts: From Product-Centric to Value-Centric

The 21st century has witnessed a notable shift from merely product-centric approaches to those that focus on providing value. Companies and marketers that have succeeded in recent times are those that offer not just products but also educational content, community support, and a sense of belonging.

Conclusion

Understanding the historical underpinnings of network marketing is not an exercise in nostalgia. Instead, it serves as a compass, illuminating the path traversed, the challenges surmounted, and providing clues for future trajectories. As Maxwell Bridge posits in this extensive guide, by embracing the lessons from the past, we stand better equipped to navigate the future, ensuring we don't fall into the same pitfalls that ensnared many before us.

Evolution of the Industry

The annals of network marketing paint a vibrant tapestry of innovation, resilience, and adaptability. This landscape, like any robust ecosystem, has been in a state of continuous evolution. Its journey from its nascent stages to its present multifaceted avatar has been marked by several transformative epochs. To truly appreciate the intricacies of the current network marketing domain, we must undertake an analytical odyssey through its evolutionary trajectory.

1. The Infancy: Direct Selling Emerges

As previously highlighted, the cradle of network marketing can be traced back to **direct selling**. Brands like Avon, in the late 19th century, pioneered a personalized approach, emphasizing human connection and trust. It was a period characterized by one-on-one interactions, primarily in physical spaces like homes, where products were showcased and sold.

2. The Adolescence: Birth of the Multi-Level Marketing (MLM) Structure

By mid-20th century, the seeds of the **MLM structure** were sown. A paradigm shift from the traditional model, this ushered in the concept of not just selling, but also recruiting. Companies like Tupperware not only sold storage containers but also built communities through Tupperware parties. By introducing the recruitment model, where sellers could bring in other sellers and earn commissions from their sales, the MLM structure amplified earning potential.

Table 1: Evolution of Network Marketing Structures

Tab. 2: Evolution of Network Marketing Structures

Era	Model	Features
Late 19th Century	Direct Selling	- One-on-One Interactions - Emphasis on Personal Relationships
Mid-20th Century	MLM	- Earnings from Direct Sales - Commissions from Recruits' Sales

3. The Young Adulthood: Rise of the Global Giants

The latter half of the 20th century saw the rise of global behemoths in network marketing. Companies like Herbalife, Nu Skin, and Amway began expanding across borders, aided in part by favorable global trade policies and the globalization wave. This was an era where network marketing started shedding its localized cloak, embracing a more globalized outlook.

4. The Digital Revolution: Network Marketing Enters Cyberspace

As the 21st century dawned, the digital revolution transformed nearly every industry, and network marketing was no exception. This period saw a seismic shift from offline to **online marketing strategies**. Personal websites, blogs, and later, social media platforms, became the new frontier. The era of digital network marketing emphasized the need for personal branding, digital literacy, and adaptability.

5. The Age of Informed Skepticism

Post the digital revolution, information became more accessible. This led to heightened scrutiny and, in many instances, skepticism. Pyramid schemes masquerading as MLMs were exposed, leading to a phase where transparency and ethics became paramount. The industry, responding to this informed skepticism, began placing greater emphasis on **education** and **authenticity**, with many companies offering detailed training programs for their affiliates.

6. The Contemporary Era: Diversification and Specialization

The present phase of network marketing is characterized by both diversification and specialization. While health and wellness remain dominant niches, we see a surge in specialized fields ranging from sustainable products to tech tools. Furthermore, companies have begun to prioritize community building, leveraging technology to foster connections, offer continuous learning, and enhance support structures.

7. Future Glimpses: Towards Sustainable and Ethical Network Marketing

Given the global emphasis on sustainability and ethical business practices, the future of network marketing seems poised to lean heavily into these areas. As Maxwell Bridge elucidates throughout this guide, understanding these evolutionary trends is key to anticipating future shifts, thereby ensuring prolonged success in the domain.

Conclusion

The evolution of network marketing is a testament to the industry's resilience and its ability to adapt to external socio-economic, technological, and cultural influences. With this detailed historical context, we are better positioned to grasp the contemporary challenges and opportunities, laying a robust foundation for the ensuing chapters. Maxwell Bridge, through his vast experience, underscores the significance of understanding this evolutionary journey, as it offers invaluable lessons for both novices and seasoned professionals in the field.

Current Trends and Predictions

Standing on the precipice of the current age, the network marketing landscape is akin to a vast ocean of opportunities, tempered by waves of challenges and shifting currents. The present, influenced by our digital age and a globalized economy, showcases a confluence of both tested strategies and innovative practices. Drawing upon **Maxwell Bridge's** decade-long expertise, let's delve into the major trends of today and forecast the shifts on the horizon.

1. Digital Dominance: The Virtual Marketplace

It's irrefutable: the digital realm has drastically altered the way network marketers operate. Recent data suggests that over **85%** of network marketing engagements now start online, with platforms like Instagram, Facebook, and LinkedIn becoming indispensable tools for recruitment and product showcasing.

Tab. 3: Digital Platform Utilization Rates (2021)

Platform	Percentage Utilization
Instagram	45%
Facebook	30%
LinkedIn	10%
Others	15%

However, this trend isn't plateauing; it's evolving. We predict a surge in the use of emerging platforms, like TikTok or Clubhouse, as marketers seek more engaging ways to connect with a younger, dynamic audience.

2. Personalization Over Generalization

In the era of data analytics, generic marketing pitches are passé. Marketers now have tools to understand individual consumer preferences, tailoring pitches and products to resonate on a personal level. Companies integrating **AI-driven analytics** into their strategies are witnessing a significant uptick in engagement rates, with some reporting improvements by up to 40%.

3. Sustainable and Ethical Practices Gain Ground

The modern consumer is well-informed and discerning. There's a clear inclination towards brands emphasizing sustainability and ethical business practices. Network marketing companies promoting eco-friendly products or those upholding fair trade standards are reporting higher customer loyalty scores, and we predict this trend to amplify in the coming years.

4. Niche Markets Take Center Stage

Gone are the days when broad-spectrum products ruled the roost. The present and future belong to specialized products catering to niche markets. Whether it's keto-friendly health supplements or tech tools for remote workers, specificity is emerging as the new buzzword.

5. Emphasis on Skill Development and Continuous Learning

The rapidly changing landscape necessitates that marketers remain perennial students. Companies are heavily investing in training programs, with a focus on digital literacy, soft skills, and market analytics. Marketers adept in these areas will likely dominate the field.

6. Predictions for the Near Future

Rise of Decentralized Platforms: With the increasing popularity of decentralized technologies, we foresee a potential shift towards decentralized platforms for network marketing, emphasizing transparency and direct peer-to-peer interactions.

Virtual Reality (VR) and Augmented Reality (AR) Integration: As technology advances, the integration of VR and AR in product demos and interactive marketing experiences might become commonplace.

Greater Regulatory Oversight: As the industry continues to grow, we can anticipate stricter regulatory measures to prevent malpractices and ensure consumer protection.

Shift Towards Health and Well-Being: Given the post-pandemic global emphasis on health, products related to wellness, mental health, and fitness will likely witness exponential growth.

Conclusion

In encapsulating the current trends and potential trajectories, it's clear that network marketing, while rooted in its core principles of personal connection and trust, is rapidly morphing to integrate modern tools, technologies, and societal shifts. Maxwell Bridge, in his signature insightful manner, reminds us that while trends change, the key to success lies in adaptability, continuous learning, and unwavering commitment to ethical practices.

Chapter 2
Common Missteps in Network Marketing

Misunderstanding the Business Model

Network marketing, colloquially known as multi-level marketing or direct selling, rests on a foundational business model that is both straightforward in concept yet intricate in execution. A fundamental grasp of this model is paramount to success, and **Maxwell Bridge's** extensive experience suggests that a majority of failures in the domain can be traced back to its misunderstanding.

1. The Basic Premise

At its core, network marketing involves selling products directly to the end consumer without a fixed retail location, leveraging word-of-mouth to procure both customers and potential new sales representatives. The structure allows representatives to earn not just from their direct sales but also from the sales made by their recruits.

Tab. 4: Traditional vs. Network Marketing Sales Flow

	Traditional Retail	**Network Marketing**
Product Procurement	Manufacturer > Wholesaler	Manufacturer > Representative
Product Sale	Retailer > Customer	Representative > Customer
Revenue Stream	Product Sales	Product Sales + Recruit's Sales

While this dual revenue stream model may appear lucrative, it's here that many aspirants falter, often prioritizing recruitment over actual sales.

2. The Misconceptions

Recruitment Over Sales: One of the most pervasive misconceptions is the overemphasis on recruitment. New representatives often operate under the illusion that recruiting more people under them is the golden ticket. In reality, without an emphasis on actual product sales, the entire structure risks becoming unsustainable, mirroring the notorious 'pyramid schemes' that have tainted the industry's reputation.

Passive Income Mirage: Another prevalent misunderstanding is that network marketing is a ticket to quick, passive income. Though there are indeed residual income opportunities, they come after establishing a robust sales network, which demands time, effort, and persistence.

3. The Subtleties of the Model

Product Value Proposition: It's imperative to understand the value proposition of the products being sold. Representatives must genuinely believe in the benefits and value of their offerings. Authentic belief drives genuine sales pitches, which, in turn, are more likely to resonate with potential customers.

The Compounding Effect: Network marketing rewards consistent effort. Regular, small sales and recruitments, over time, can lead to a compounding effect, exponentially increasing income.

4. The Pitfalls of Misunderstanding

Misunderstanding the model can lead to:

- **Unsustainable Business Practices:** Over-focusing on recruitment can result in a fragile network with shallow roots, prone to collapsing.

- **Reputation Damage:** Inauthentic sales pitches or aggressive recruitment can tarnish individual and industry-wide reputations.

- **Financial Strain:** Misaligned expectations can result in significant financial investments without commensurate returns, causing monetary strain.

Conclusion

To navigate the vast ocean of network marketing successfully, one must first understand the ship they're sailing – the business model. It's neither about merely selling products nor just about recruiting; it's an intricate dance between the two, balanced on the fulcrum of genuine value delivery.

As Maxwell Bridge eloquently emphasizes throughout this guide, the key to thriving in network marketing lies in comprehending its nuances and operating from a place of authenticity and genuine belief in the product's value. By sidestepping the common pitfalls of misunderstanding, one can lay a robust foundation for long-term success.

Over-reliance on a Single Strategy

Network marketing, as **Maxwell Bridge** often elucidates throughout this opus, is a multi-faceted domain, reflecting the diversity and dynamism of the markets it operates within. Given the multifarious nature of this industry, an adherence to a singular strategy can, unfortunately, be tantamount to tunnel vision—a narrowing of focus that often precedes a fall.

1. The Perils of Monolithic Approaches

In a world characterized by rapid technological, sociological, and economic shifts, clinging to a solitary strategy reflects not just a rigidity of approach but also a disconnect from the evolving external environment.

Tab. 5: Single vs. Diverse Strategy Approach

	Single Strategy	Diverse Strategy
Adaptability	Low	High
Risk Exposure	High	Spread Out/Diversified
Market Coverage	Narrow	Wide
Longevity	Short-term	Sustainable Long-term

The pitfalls of such an over-reliance include:

- **Missed Opportunities:** Other potentially profitable avenues remain unexplored, leading to lost potential gains.

- **Higher Vulnerability:** A strategy, no matter how effective, might become obsolete or less effective over time. Relying solely on it can expose one to greater risks.

- **Stagnation:** In an evolving landscape, stasis is synonymous with regression. A singular strategy can lead to stagnation, both in terms of business growth and personal development.

2. Historical Precedents

History is replete with examples from various industries where an over-reliance on one successful strategy led to eventual downfall. Kodak's over-reliance on film photography despite the rise of digital imaging or Blockbuster's focus on physical rental stores ignoring the shift to digital streaming serve as somber reminders.

3. The Network Marketing Context

In the realm of network marketing:

- **Product-Centric Strategy:** Overemphasis on a single product, disregarding shifts in market needs or emerging competition, can result in dwindling sales.

- **Single Channel Focus:** Exclusively relying on, say, face-to-face interactions, ignoring the rise of digital platforms, can lead to reduced outreach.

- **One-Size-Fits-All Pitch:** Not customizing your pitch to cater to diverse segments of the population can limit potential conversions.

4. Embracing Versatility: The Path Forward

It's not about discarding what's working but augmenting it with additional strategies. Diversifying doesn't mean dilution. It's about building a resilient, flexible approach that can weather market fluctuations and tap into emerging opportunities.

Steps towards a versatile approach:

- **Continuous Learning:** Stay updated with the latest trends in the industry. This will allow timely identification and adoption of successful strategies.

- **Feedback Mechanism:** Establish a robust feedback mechanism to continuously assess and adapt your strategies based on real-world results.

- **Collaborate:** Networking isn't just about sales; it's also about learning from peers. Engage with fellow network marketers, attend seminars, and participate in workshops.

Conclusion

In the articulate words of **Maxwell Bridge**, "Versatility isn't an option; it's a necessity." In the intricate tapestry of network marketing, a monochromatic approach can seldom capture the vast array of opportunities that lie woven within. Diversifying strategies ensures not only the maximization of these opportunities but also shields one against unforeseeable market vicissitudes. As the adage goes, "Don't put all your eggs in one basket." In network marketing, this couldn't be truer.

Failing to Evolve with the Industry

It's a fundamental truth across any business discipline: adaptation is not an option; it's a survival imperative. The dictum is especially poignant in the landscape of network marketing, an industry characterized by rapid evolution and frequent paradigm shifts. **Maxwell Bridge**, with his rich tapestry of experience, has perennially emphasized the role of evolution in a marketer's journey. *Adapt, or become obsolete* is more than a cautionary refrain; it's an operational mantra for anyone seeking success in this domain.

1. The Historical Context

Revisiting the annals of network marketing reveals a series of transformational milestones. From the door-to-door salesmanship of the 50s to the advent of internet-based networking in the late 90s, each epoch demanded a recalibration of strategies and tools.

2. The Cost of Stasis

Resisting change, consciously or otherwise, often incurs:

- **Diminishing Returns:** Continuation with outdated methods results in progressively reduced efficacy.

- **Lost Competitive Edge:** As competitors embrace and optimize new strategies, those who don't evolve find themselves left behind.

- **Reputational Costs:** Modern clients and partners seek dynamic, forward-thinking collaborators. Sticking to old methodologies can be perceived as rigidity, denting one's brand image.

3. Contemporary Evolutionary Forces

Modern network marketing isn't what it was even a decade ago. The rise of social media, advancements in customer relationship management software, and sophisticated data analytics tools have revolutionized outreach, engagement, and conversion strategies.

Tab. 6: Evolutionary Milestones in the 21st Century

Year	Evolutionary Force	Impact on Network Marketing
2005	Rise of Social Media	Expanded outreach; Direct customer engagement
2010	Mobile Marketing	Personalized targeting; Geo-specific marketing
2015	Big Data & Analytics	Informed decision-making; Predictive marketing
2020	AI & Machine Learning	Automated workflows; Enhanced customer experience

4. Navigating Evolution: A Guide

Embracing change requires more than intent; it demands a systematic, strategic approach:

- **Continuous Learning:** Keep abreast with the industry's latest trends, tools, and best practices. Whether through formal training, webinars, or workshops, one must remain an eternal student.

- **Feedback Loops:** Establish channels to receive and act upon feedback from team members, customers, and partners. Feedback is the compass that guides evolutionary journeys.

- **Collaborative Evolution:** Engage in think-tanks, attend industry conclaves, and be a part of online forums. Collective intelligence can often spotlight evolutionary forces before they become mainstream.

5. Evolution as a Mindset

Maxwell Bridge has, time and again, underlined the importance of cultivating a growth mindset. To evolve isn't merely to adopt new tools or strategies. It's to foster a mindset that seeks, welcomes, and integrates change as a natural aspect of professional life.

Conclusion

In the intricate ballet of network marketing, failing to evolve isn't just a misstep; it's a recipe for obsolescence. The industry, with its pulse on societal, technological, and market dynamics, demands a symphony of adaptive maneuvers from its participants. To paraphrase **Maxwell Bridge**'s sagacious counsel, "In the world of network marketing, evolution isn't a phase; it's the very essence."

Neglecting Personal Development

"To stand still is to regress" - this adage, profound in its simplicity, encapsulates the peril of neglecting personal development, especially in an industry as dynamic as network marketing. Personal development isn't merely an aspect of professional growth; it's the very bedrock upon which a successful network marketing career is built. Maxwell Bridge's astute insights, drawn from his decade-long journey, consistently emphasize that individuals often falter in network marketing not because of external challenges but due to an internal inertia.

1. The Cruciality of Personal Development

The network marketing domain is essentially a people-driven industry. It demands skills beyond the rudimentary understanding of products or sales techniques. Building rapport, understanding consumer psychologies, fostering lasting relationships, and leading teams - these abilities aren't innate; they are cultivated.

2. The Dichotomy of Growth

It's imperative to distinguish between two parallel growth trajectories in network marketing:

- **External Growth:** This encompasses expanding networks, higher sales volumes, and tangible metrics that usually define success.

- **Internal Growth:** This is about the evolution of an individual - sharpening soft skills, enhancing emotional intelligence, cultivating leadership qualities, and continuously updating oneself with industry knowledge.

Neglecting the latter invariably stunts the former.

3. Symptoms of Neglected Development

Several markers indicate an inertia in personal growth:

- **Stagnation in Network Growth:** An inability to expand or even maintain networks suggests that one might not be evolving at the pace the industry demands.

- **Decreasing Sales Efficacy:** If earlier strategies now yield diminishing returns, it may reflect a disconnect with current market dynamics.

- **Intra-team Conflicts:** Leadership isn't about management but about inspiration. Dissonance within teams can signal a leadership development lag.

4. Catalysts for Personal Evolution

To break the inertia and reignite the spirit of self-evolution:

- **Regular Training:** Deliberate efforts to upgrade industry-specific skills ensure one stays in tune with the latest trends and techniques.

- **Soft Skills Workshops:** From communication to conflict resolution, soft skills often determine the difference between mediocre and exceptional.

- **Mentorship:** Engaging with industry leaders, or even cross-industry mentors, can offer invaluable perspectives.

- **Feedback Mechanisms:** Constructive criticism is a growth agent. It's crucial to institute mechanisms, formal or informal, to receive feedback and act upon it.

Tab. 7: Personal Development Metrics & Corresponding Outcomes

Personal Development Metric	Corresponding Outcome in Network Marketing
Hours of Soft Skills Training	Enhanced Relationship Building
Number of Books Read/Year	Broadened Perspective & Innovative Strategies
Mentorship Engagements/Month	Guided & Informed Decision Making
Regular Feedback Sessions	Streamlined Processes & Continuous Improvement

5. Personal Development as an Investment

Every hour dedicated to personal development translates into tangible returns in network marketing. Maxwell Bridge often likens this to the most profitable investment one can make in this industry. It's not just about immediate gains, but long-term dividends. A commitment to perpetual learning and growth not only elevates personal efficacy but also enhances brand perception.

Conclusion

In the panoramic vista of network marketing, where success is often gauged by metrics, numbers, and growth charts, it's easy to overlook the most significant metric of all - personal evolution. As

Maxwell Bridge sagely counsels, "In this industry, you are your most significant asset. Invest in yourself, nurture your growth, and the external metrics will inevitably follow."

Chapter 3
The Mindset Challenge

The Pitfalls of a Fixed Mindset

In the intricate dance of network marketing, where strategy, skill, and even serendipity play pivotal roles, it's easy to overlook the significance of one's mindset. At the heart of success, or the lack thereof, is often not what one does, but how one thinks. Delving deep into this cognitive dimension, Maxwell Bridge's insights, gleaned from over a decade of navigating the tumultuous terrains of network marketing, reveal a compelling narrative: the detriments of harboring a fixed mindset.

1. Understanding the Fixed Mindset

Carol Dweck, in her groundbreaking research, delineated the dichotomy of **fixed and growth mindsets**. A fixed mindset, as the nomenclature suggests, is rooted in static beliefs about oneself. Such an individual perceives their abilities, intelligence, and talents as fixed traits, inherently capped and immutable. In the realm of network marketing, this translates to a perception of static potential - a ceiling on growth, learning, and adaptability.

2. How a Fixed Mindset Manifests in Network Marketing

Several symptomatic manifestations of a fixed mindset can be identified in the professional behaviors of network marketers:

- **Reluctance to Adapt:** A reluctance to embrace new strategies, tools, or technologies, stemming from a belief that past successes determine future outcomes.

- **Fear of Failure:** An aversion to risks, given the assumption that failures are not just setbacks but reflect one's inherent and unchangeable lack of competence.

- **Defensiveness:** A propensity to resist feedback, viewing it as a personal affront rather than an opportunity for growth.

- **Comparative Evaluation:** A continual comparison with peers, leading to either complacency (when ahead) or despondency (when trailing).

3. The Consequences of a Fixed Mindset in Network Marketing

The repercussions of a fixed mindset extend beyond personal stagnation. They have tangible, often deleterious, outcomes:

- **Missed Opportunities:** A failure to recognize or seize potential growth avenues due to a myopic view of one's capacities.

- **Reduced Resilience:** An inability to bounce back from setbacks, given the deep-seated belief that challenges are insurmountable for someone with 'limited' abilities.

- **Diminished Team Morale:** Leadership rooted in a fixed mindset can stifle team innovation, leading to disillusionment and disengagement.

- **Stunted Growth:** Ultimately, a stagnant career trajectory, as newer, more adaptable competitors harness opportunities.

Tab. 8: Fixed Mindset vs. Growth Mindset in Network Marketing

Trait	Fixed Mindset	Growth Mindset
View on Challenges	Threats	Opportunities
Reaction to Failure	Defeat	Learning Opportunity
Approach to Feedback	Defensive	Welcoming
Perception of Effort	Fruitless	Path to Mastery

4. The Underlying Psychology

It's critical to understand that a fixed mindset isn't an inherent flaw but often a conditioned response. Past failures, societal conditioning, or even early educational experiences can entrench this mindset. Recognizing these triggers is the first step towards transformation.

5. Breaking Free from the Fixed Mindset

Liberating oneself from the shackles of a fixed mindset is neither instant nor effortless. It demands introspection, sustained effort, and often, external guidance. Maxwell Bridge accentuates the value of mentors, continuous learning, and open-mindedness in this transformative journey.

Conclusion

In an industry as dynamic and evolving as network marketing, the confines of a fixed mindset can be severely restrictive. Recognizing its pitfalls, understanding its origins, and embarking on a deliberate journey towards a growth-oriented mindset can be the fulcrum upon which success pivots. As Maxwell Bridge astutely observes, "In network marketing, it's not always the most skilled who succeed, but the most adaptable."

Embracing a Growth Mindset: Why It's Crucial

In the echoing corridors of corporate culture, the term "growth mindset" has swiftly transcended from being a mere buzzword to a fundamental ethos guiding innovation, adaptation, and success. Distinguished psychologist Dr. Carol Dweck's research on the transformative power of viewing challenges as stepping stones rather than stumbling blocks has been revolutionary. In network marketing, where adaptability, continuous learning, and personal evolution are paramount, adopting a growth mindset isn't just beneficial—it's imperative.

1. Decoding the Growth Mindset

A **growth mindset** can be best understood in contrast to its counterpart, the fixed mindset. Individuals with a growth mindset believe that abilities and intelligence can be developed with dedication, effort, and the right strategies. They are more inclined to embrace challenges, persist during setbacks, and see effort as a path to improvement. It's not about being optimistic but being open, adaptable, and relentless.

2. Significance in Network Marketing

In the fluctuating arena of network marketing, a growth mindset emerges as a beacon, illuminating:

- **Adaptability:** Network marketing is in perpetual motion. New techniques, platforms, and paradigms emerge routinely. Embracing these changes, rather than resisting them, can be the determinant of success or stagnation.

- **Resilience:** The inevitable rejections, setbacks, and hurdles encountered in network marketing can be daunting. A growth mindset transforms these challenges into learning opportunities, bolstering perseverance.

- **Continuous Learning:** The landscape of network marketing is nuanced. There's always a new skill to master, a new strategy to deploy. Those armed with a growth mindset are ever-eager learners, always seeking ways to enhance their craft.

3. The Far-reaching Implications of a Growth Mindset

Beyond mere professional implications, a growth mindset has profound personal repercussions:

- **Enhanced Well-being:** Embracing challenges and viewing setbacks as learning opportunities fosters positivity and reduces stress and anxiety.

- **Empowered Relationships:** This mindset extends to viewing interpersonal challenges as opportunities for growth and understanding, fostering richer, more fulfilling relationships.

- **Personal Evolution:** As Maxwell Bridge posits, "In embracing growth, you don't just evolve in your career, you evolve as a person."

4. Cultivating a Growth Mindset

Recognizing the value of a growth mindset is one thing, actively cultivating it is another. Some strategies to consider:

- **Embrace Challenges:** Instead of avoiding challenges, see them as valuable growth opportunities.

- **Redefine 'Failure':** View setbacks not as proof of incompetence but as essential feedback.

- **Learn Actively:** Engage in training, read extensively, and always seek opportunities to enhance your skill set.

- **Seek Constructive Feedback:** Embrace external perspectives as a means to identify growth areas.

Tab. 9: Shifting Perspectives: Fixed vs. Growth Mindset in Network Marketing

Situation	Fixed Mindset Reaction	Growth Mindset Reaction
A New Challenge	Avoidance due to fear of failure	Excitement due to potential learning
Feedback	A personal attack or affront	An opportunity to improve
Setbacks	Proof of lack of ability	An avenue for reflection and growth
Success of Peers	A threat or source of jealousy	An inspiration and a source of learning

5. Conclusion

The volatile realm of network marketing demands more than just strategic acumen and interpersonal skills. It demands a mindset wired for growth, evolution, and relentless learning. As Maxwell Bridge sagely points out, "Your mindset isn't just about thinking; it's the bedrock of your actions, reactions, and ultimately, your results in the network marketing industry."

By mastering the growth mindset, network marketers not only set themselves up for professional success but also embark on a journey of personal evolution, enhancing every facet of their lives.

Overcoming Negative Stereotypes and Bias

While the network marketing domain has evolved into a legitimate business model, its history is not devoid of shadows. From early misconceptions to genuine misconduct by a handful of practitioners, these shadows have fostered a repertoire of negative stereotypes and biases. In this environment, the network marketer's battle is not merely against market dynamics, but against deeply entrenched societal perceptions. Drawing insights from Maxwell Bridge's vast experience, this segment delineates the nature of these stereotypes, their origins, and provides a structured roadmap to effectively challenge and overcome them.

1. Understanding the Root of Stereotypes

Network marketing, unfortunately, has often been conflated with *pyramid schemes*, thereby sowing the seeds of distrust. Pyramid schemes are illicit and unsustainable, primarily enriching those at the top at the expense of those at the bottom. Network marketing, in contrast, revolves around genuine products and services, rewarding based on sales and team-building.

2. Common Stereotypes and Their Impact

- **Overzealous Recruiters:** The aggressive recruitment strategy of a few has painted many with the same brush.

- **Quick-rich Schemes:** The misrepresentation of network marketing as a way to make vast sums overnight.

- **Inauthentic Interactions:** A belief that network marketers are insincere, viewing every interaction as a sales opportunity.

These stereotypes, while based on the actions of a minority, cast a shadow over the entire industry, often causing genuine professionals to face undue skepticism and distrust.

3. The Psychological Mechanics of Bias

Humans are predisposed to **cognitive shortcuts**, simplifying complex information into digestible chunks. While efficient, this process is prone to distortion. When negative experiences or stories related to network marketing become widely circulated, they feed into the collective consciousness, reinforcing and amplifying biases.

Tab. 10: Cognitive Biases in Network Marketing

Bias Type	Description	Impact on Network Marketing Perception
Confirmation Bias	Favoring information that confirms existing beliefs	Reinforces negative stereotypes once they are accepted
Availability Heuristic	Relying on immediate examples when evaluating something	Recent negative stories can overshadow years of positive experiences
Stereotype Anchoring	Initial stereotypes influence subsequent perceptions	New encounters with network marketers are seen through the lens of existing biases

4. Strategies for Overcoming Stereotypes and Bias

- **Educate Proactively:** The onus is on network marketers to inform prospects about the genuine value and legitimacy of their business. Openly addressing misconceptions can disarm skeptics.

- **Model Authenticity:** Relationships should be built on trust and sincerity. Authentic interactions devoid of ulterior motives can counter the stereotype of inauthenticity.

- **Transparency:** Clear communication about business models, compensation structures, and product value can dispel myths. The more transparent you are, the less room there is for doubt.

- **Engage in Ethical Marketing:** Avoiding exaggerated claims or aggressive tactics will set you apart and help reshape the narrative.

- **Leverage Testimonials:** Real stories from satisfied customers or team members can challenge existing narratives and provide credible counterexamples.

- **Continuous Personal Development:** Maxwell Bridge emphasizes the importance of personal growth in network marketing. By enhancing soft skills like communication, empathy, and active listening, one can navigate biases more effectively.

5. Conclusion

Negative stereotypes and biases are daunting, but they are not insurmountable. As network marketers, understanding these perceptions, their origins, and their implications is the first step. The subsequent challenge lies in proactive education, genuine relationship-building, and an unwavering commitment to ethical practices.

Drawing from Maxwell Bridge's wisdom, it becomes evident that while external biases exist, the true power to redefine network marketing's narrative lies inherently within each practitioner. The journey to reshape perceptions begins with each interaction, each transaction, and each genuine connection.

Building Resilience in the Face of Rejection

Rejection, a ubiquitous element within the universe of network marketing, often holds an unwarranted amount of power over an individual's psyche. Resilience, defined as the capacity to recover quickly from adversities, becomes paramount in this arena. *Maxwell Bridge*, leveraging his extensive voyage through the highs and lows of the industry, provides a comprehensive understanding and strategy for nurturing resilience, especially when confronted with the inevitable: rejection.

1. The Nature and Psychology of Rejection

Rejection, in the context of network marketing, can range from a declined product pitch to a potential recruit's decision against joining your team. The sting of rejection is rooted in our evolutionary biology; historically, rejection from a tribe or community meant vulnerability to threats. In the modern context, it translates into self-doubt and impacts our self-worth.

2. Rejection in Network Marketing: A Different Beast

In conventional industries, rejection may be intermittent. However, in network marketing, with its foundation on personal interactions and pitches, rejection can be a frequent companion. This frequent interaction with rejection requires not just thick skin, but a mindset that sees rejection as a stepping stone rather than a blockade.

Tab. 11: Types of Rejections in Network Marketing

Type	Description	Potential Impact
Product Rejection	Decline of the product being pitched	Loss of potential sale
Recruitment Rejection	Potential recruits deciding against joining	Missed team expansion opportunity
Relationship Rejection	Breakdown in existing team relationships or clientele	Loss of established network and potential revenue

3. Building Resilience: A Methodical Approach

- **Reframe Rejection:** Instead of viewing rejection as a failure, consider it feedback. Every rejection offers insights into areas of potential improvement.

50

- **Limit Emotional Contagion:** Emotions are contagious. Surrounding oneself with positive, forward-thinking individuals can shield against the pessimism that often accompanies rejection.

- **Mindfulness and Meditation:** Engaging in mindfulness practices can enhance emotional regulation, aiding in quicker recovery from the initial sting of rejection.

- **Establish a Support System:** This could be in the form of mentors, peers, or even training programs. Knowing that there is a safety net can significantly alleviate the fear of rejection.

- **Celebrate Small Wins:** While it's essential to have long-term goals, celebrating incremental achievements can provide the necessary motivation and counterbalance against the impacts of rejection.

4. Tools for Resilience

Visualization Techniques: Before entering a potentially rejection-prone situation, visualize a positive outcome. Even if the result deviates from this visualization, the proactive positive reinforcement can buffer against negativity.

Feedback Loops: Instead of dwelling on the rejection, seek feedback. Understand the 'why' behind the rejection. This constructive approach can turn potential pitfalls into learning opportunities.

5. The Ripple Effect of Resilience

Building resilience does more than just aid in handling rejection. It spills over into other areas:

- **Enhanced Productivity:** A resilient mindset, less bogged down by rejection, can focus more on action and results.

- **Better Relationships:** Resilient individuals often radiate positivity, fostering healthier team dynamics and client relationships.

- **Innovation and Adaptability:** When not paralyzed by the fear of rejection, one becomes more open to trying new strategies, leading to innovation.

6. Conclusion

In the ever-challenging world of network marketing, rejection is not merely a possibility but a guarantee. Drawing from the wisdom of *Maxwell Bridge*, it becomes evident that the difference between success and stagnation often lies not in the rejection itself but in one's response to it. Cultivating resilience, thus, is not just a strategy but a necessity. With resilience as an ally, every rejection becomes a step forward, not backward, on the path to network marketing success.

Chapter 4
Building Your Brand

Why Personal Branding is Vital

In the modern digital age, an era characterized by rapid information exchange and heightened interconnectivity, **personal branding** has emerged as an indispensable asset. Within the domain of network marketing, this rings particularly true. At the heart of this industry lies the principle of building and nurturing relationships. As *Maxwell Bridge* astutely observed through his decade-long journey, success in this sector is intimately tethered to one's ability to authentically portray oneself, forge genuine connections, and establish trust.

1. Defining Personal Branding

Personal branding is a strategic process of creating a distinctive and consistent image and reputation that people remember and resonate with. It's the perception or emotion maintained by customers, stakeholders, or colleagues when they think of you.

2. The Changing Landscape of Network Marketing and the Rise of Personal Branding

With the saturation of products and services in the market, consumers have grown wary of generic pitches. The modern consumer seeks more than just a product; they seek an experience, a story, and most importantly, a genuine human connection.

3. The Benefits of Personal Branding in Network Marketing

- **Differentiation in a Crowded Market:** In an industry teeming with similar products and replicated pitches, a strong personal brand helps one stand out. It's your unique signature in the market.

- **Building Trust and Credibility:** Personal branding elevates your status from a mere seller to a trusted consultant. People buy from those they trust.

- **Loyalty and Retention:** Customers aligned with your brand values and persona are more likely to remain loyal, ensuring sustainable revenue streams.

- **Increased Referral Rates:** A strong personal brand often leads to word-of-mouth referrals, amplifying sales without additional marketing spend.

Tab. 12: Impact of Personal Branding on Business Metrics

Metrics	Without Personal Branding	With Personal Branding
Customer Retention	40%	70%
Referral Rate	10%	50%
Trust Score	5/10	8/10

The table highlights how personal branding can quantifiably elevate various business metrics, leading to overall business growth.

4. The Crucial Elements of Personal Branding

- **Authenticity:** The foundation of personal branding. Presenting a genuine version of oneself fosters trust.

- **Consistency:** Your brand should provide consistency across all touchpoints, from social media to face-to-face interactions.

- **Value Proposition:** Clearly communicating what you offer and how it differentiates you from others.

- **Engagement:** Actively engaging with your audience to nurture relationships and gather feedback.

- **Storytelling:** Weaving your personal journey and experiences into a relatable narrative that resonates with your audience.

5. Challenges and Misconceptions

Despite its evident advantages, personal branding isn't devoid of challenges:

- **Over-commercialization:** Striking a balance between being genuine and turning oneself into a mere marketing tool.

- **Maintaining Authenticity:** The temptation to mould oneself to market demands can compromise authenticity.

- **Time and Effort:** Building a brand doesn't happen overnight. It demands consistent effort and adaptability.

6. Conclusion

In the intricate dance of network marketing, where relationships and trust form the stage, personal branding emerges as the choreography that can enchant the audience. Drawing from *Maxwell Bridge's* profound insights, it becomes abundantly clear that to truly excel in network marketing, one must invest not just in products or strategies, but in oneself. For, in the end, people don't just buy a product, they buy 'you'.

Crafting Your Unique Selling Proposition (USP)

Network marketing, as *Maxwell Bridge* astutely observes through a lens of rigorous experience, is not simply about selling products or services—it's about selling oneself. The commoditization of numerous product lines and services has made differentiation in the market increasingly challenging. Yet, a fundamental differentiator still remains: the individual network marketer themselves. And at the heart of this differentiation is the **Unique Selling Proposition (USP)**.

1. Understanding the Unique Selling Proposition (USP)

The USP is a succinct, clear, and compelling message that conveys why a potential client or partner should choose you over competitors. It addresses what makes you, as a network marketer, distinctively valuable in a saturated market. A well-crafted USP transcends mere product characteristics—it touches upon your values, your approach, and the unique experience of collaborating with you.

2. Crafting a Magnetic USP: A Structured Approach

- **Self-Reflection and Analysis:** Begin by introspecting about your strengths, values, passions, and experiences. What personal narrative or journey sets you apart? For many in the industry, their unique tales of transformation often become the core of their USP.

- **Understanding the Audience:** Delve deep into the psyche of your target audience. What are their pain points, aspirations, and desires? A resonant USP speaks directly to these.

- **Marrying Personal Strengths with Audience Needs:** Your USP should be an amalgamation of what you uniquely offer and what your audience earnestly seeks.

Tab. 13: Crafting the USP: An Intersectional Analysis

Your Strengths/Values	Audience Needs/Pain Points	Potential USP
Personal Transformation Experience	Looking for Genuine Success Stories	"From struggle to success: Let's journey together."
Ethical Product Sourcing	Ethical Consumption	"Products with a conscience for the conscientious consumer."
Extensive Training Programs	Need for Skill Development	"Empowerment through education: I grow when you grow."

This table showcases how an intersectional analysis can yield compelling USP statements.

3. Testing and Refinement

Once a tentative USP is developed, it's crucial to test it among a sample group—colleagues, mentors, or a subset of potential clients. Gather feedback, understand its impact, and refine accordingly.

4. Incorporating the USP Across Touchpoints

An effective USP is not just to be spoken or written—it's to be lived and exhibited. Integrate it across:

- **Personal Interactions:** Be it a sales pitch or casual networking, ensure your USP essence is consistently communicated.

- **Digital Platforms:** Your websites, social media profiles, and email signatures should resonate with your USP.

- **Marketing Collaterals:** Brochures, business cards, or promotional materials should all carry a clear imprint of your USP.

5. Challenges in USP Development

- **Overgeneralization:** Many network marketers fall into the trap of making their USP too broad, rendering it ineffective.

- **Overcomplication:** A USP that's too complex can alienate the target audience. Simplicity often leads to better recall and resonance.

- **Static Mindset:** As the market evolves, there might be a need to tweak or entirely revamp the USP. Being adaptable is crucial.

6. Conclusion

In the grand theater of network marketing, where individuality is the most significant asset one can leverage, the USP becomes the script that commands attention. Drawing from the profound insights of *Maxwell Bridge*, we discern that a potent USP is not just about selling—it's about captivating, resonating, and building an indelible mark in the minds of your audience. It's more than a statement—it's your signature.

Consistency in Brand Representation

In the grand tapestry of network marketing, there exists a thread so foundational, yet so often overlooked, that its absence or inconsistency can fray the very fabric of success. This thread, dear reader, is the consistency in brand representation. As *Maxwell Bridge* opines, with the authority lent by his extensive experience, a brand in the network marketing domain is not just a name or logo; it is an ethos, an experience, and most critically, a promise. Consistency in its representation is not just a best practice—it's a non-negotiable imperative.

1. The Pillars of Brand Consistency

Brands are built on several pillars, each demanding unwavering consistency:

- **Visual Identity:** This includes logos, color schemes, and other visual elements that create brand recognition.

- **Tonal Voice:** The style, voice, and emotion with which the brand communicates, whether in written content, visuals, or speech.

- **Core Values:** The unyielding principles guiding every action and decision.

- **Brand Promise:** The consistent delivery of value and experience promised to the customer.

Tab. 14: Pillars of Brand Consistency

Pillar	Description	Example in Network Marketing
Visual Identity	Logos, color schemes, visual elements	Using a standardized logo across all promotional materials.
Tonal Voice	Style, emotion, manner of communication	Conveying hope and empowerment in every presentation.
Core Values	Unyielding principles guiding actions	Transparency in product sourcing and selling.
Brand Promise	Consistent delivery of value and experience	Delivering reliable product quality every time.

2. The Imperative of Brand Consistency

a. Trust Building: Consistency breeds familiarity. With familiarity comes trust. When a potential client or partner encounters a consistent brand image, it reinforces their confidence in the brand's reliability.

b. Differentiation: In the sea of network marketers, many swim, but few stand out. Consistency ensures that you are not just another fish but a memorable entity.

c. Enhanced Recall: Repetition and consistency enhance brand recall, ensuring that when a client thinks of a product or service, your brand is the first to come to mind.

d. Efficient Resource Utilization: Consistent branding streamlines marketing efforts, making them more efficient and cost-effective.

3. The Risks of Inconsistency

a. Brand Dilution: Inconsistent representation weakens the brand, making it less recognizable and impactful.

b. Customer Confusion: Inconsistent messaging or visuals can confuse potential clients, leading to mistrust or disinterest.

c. Competitive Disadvantage: A consistent competitor can easily overshadow an inconsistent brand, stealing away potential clientele.

4. Implementing Brand Consistency in Network Marketing

a. Brand Guidelines: Create a comprehensive brand guideline that details visual, tonal, and core value elements. Every time a marketing material is produced, refer to this guideline.

b. Periodic Audits: Conduct regular brand audits to ensure all materials, across all platforms, remain consistent.

c. Training: Ensure that anyone representing the brand, whether they're directly associated or part of your downstream, understands and adheres to the brand's essence.

d. Feedback Loops: Establish mechanisms to gather feedback on brand representation, making adjustments as needed to ensure consistency.

5. The Dynamic Nature of Consistency

While consistency is paramount, it mustn't be mistaken for rigidity. As *Maxwell Bridge* astutely points out, brands should evolve, but such evolution should be deliberate, well-communicated, and consistent in its rollout.

6. Conclusion

Consistency in brand representation is not a mere tactic—it is a strategic imperative. In the words of *Maxwell Bridge*, "Your brand is a story unfolding across all customer touchpoints." This story, to be impactful, must be told consistently. Through consistent representation, a network marketer doesn't just sell a product or service—they sell an experience, a promise, and most importantly, a trust. It's not merely about being seen, but about being remembered.

Digital Branding: Website, Social Media, and Beyond

In the age of unprecedented digital advancement, *Maxwell Bridge* imparts that understanding and harnessing the power of digital branding stands at the vanguard of success in network marketing. In his esteemed words, "Digital branding is no longer an option; it's a necessity." The digital realm offers both challenges and opportunities for the astute network marketer. By ensuring that you harness this medium's full potential, you fortify your brand's presence, outreach, and resonance.

1. The Significance of a Well-Designed Website

The website serves as the cornerstone of your digital branding efforts. It's the virtual storefront and often the first point of contact between you and your potential clients.

- **Functionality:** Ensure your website is user-friendly, responsive (adapts to various device sizes), and has fast loading times. Remember, a frustrated user rarely becomes a client.

- **Content Quality:** Provide valuable, relevant, and consistent content. Blogs, articles, and resources related to network marketing can position you as an industry expert.

- **Search Engine Optimization (SEO):** A well-optimized website ranks higher on search engines, drawing organic traffic and increasing visibility.

- **Branding Consistency:** The visual and tonal consistency of your website with other branding materials ensures a cohesive brand image.

2. The Power of Social Media

With billions of users across platforms, social media is a veritable goldmine for network marketers.

- **Platform Selection:** Choose platforms based on your target demographic. While Instagram and TikTok might be effective for younger audiences, platforms like LinkedIn might resonate more with professionals.

- **Content Strategy:** From informational posts, success stories, to interactive content like polls or quizzes, ensure you have a varied content mix that engages users.

- **Engagement:** Responding to comments, messages, and mentions helps in building a community and fosters trust.

- **Influencer Collaborations:** Engage with influencers in the network marketing space to amplify reach.

Tab. 15: Recommended Social Media Platforms for Different Target Audiences

Audience	Platform	Content Strategy Example
Young Adults (18-24)	Instagram, TikTok	Short video testimonials, interactive stories
Adults (25-45)	Facebook, LinkedIn	Blog post shares, success stories, webinars
Professionals	LinkedIn	Whitepapers, case studies, networking events
Global Audiences	Twitter/X	News updates, industry trends, global success stories

3. Beyond Traditional Digital Platforms

As *Maxwell Bridge* has emphasized, one must always stay ahead of the curve. With that in mind, there are emerging platforms and strategies one can employ:

- **Podcasting:** This rapidly growing medium offers an opportunity to share insights, interviews, and more, reaching audiences during their commute, workouts, or downtime.

- **Webinars:** An effective tool for both education and sales, allowing real-time interaction with prospects.

- **Email Marketing:** A personalized way to keep your audience informed about the latest updates, products, and success stories.

- **Affiliate and Referral Programs:** Leverage the power of community by incentivizing referrals through digital platforms.

4. Monitoring and Analytics

No digital branding effort is complete without continuous monitoring:

- **Website Analytics:** Tools like Google Analytics provide insights into user behavior, traffic sources, and more.

- **Social Media Metrics:** Engagement rates, follower growth, and content performance metrics help refine strategy.

- **Feedback Loops:** Use surveys, feedback forms, and comments to gather user insights and adapt accordingly.

5. Conclusion

To quote *Maxwell Bridge*, "In the digital age, your brand's footprint isn't measured by the steps it takes but by the imprints it leaves in the virtual sands of the internet." As the demarcations between the real and virtual worlds blur, the efficacy of your digital branding efforts will largely determine your success trajectory in network marketing. It's not just about being present online; it's about creating ripples, building communities, fostering engagement, and most crucially, driving conversions in the vast ocean of the digital realm.

Chapter 5
Crafting an Effective Strategy

Analyzing Your Target Market

To navigate the intricate maze of network marketing successfully, understanding one's audience is paramount. As emphasized by *Maxwell Bridge*, "A product or service, no matter how excellent, is rendered futile if not matched to the correct audience." This statement underscores the dire need to dissect and comprehend one's target market meticulously. The task is not about broad categorizations but involves delving into intricate details, understanding individual preferences, and recognizing emerging patterns.

1. The Concept of a Target Market

A target market is a specific group of people most likely to be interested in your product or service. They share certain characteristics, whether demographic, psychographic, geographic, or behavioral. Analyzing this group in depth helps in tailoring marketing efforts, product offerings, and customer service strategies to resonate most effectively.

2. Steps to Identifying Your Target Market

- **Market Research:** Begin with comprehensive research. Use tools like surveys, interviews, and focus groups. Look into industry reports and studies that offer insights into market segments pertinent to network marketing.

- **Analyze Existing Customer Base:** If you've been in the business even for a short time, study your current customers. Understand why they buy from you, what resonates with them, and find common characteristics.

- **Competitor Analysis:** Identify your key competitors and analyze their target markets. This provides an insight into potential market segments that might be underserved and can be tapped into.

- **Segmentation:** Divide your target market into smaller segments based on shared characteristics. This allows for more personalized marketing strategies.

Tab. 16: Example of Market Segmentation

Segmentation Criteria	Segment	Characteristics
Demographic	Age Group: 18-30	Tech-savvy, value online testimonials, seek authenticity
Psychographic	Lifestyle: Fitness Enthusiasts	Prioritize health, active on fitness forums/apps, buy wellness products
Geographic	Region: Urban Centers	Prefer online shopping, influenced by urban trends
Behavioral	Purchase Behavior: Frequent Shoppers	Engage with regular promotions, loyal to brands they trust

3. Profiling and Persona Creation

Once the market is segmented, create detailed profiles or personas for each segment. A persona is a semi-fictional representation of your ideal customer. This involves giving them a name, a backstory, preferences, challenges, and goals. *Maxwell Bridge* often emphasizes the value of "knowing" your customer personally. It transforms an abstract marketing process into a more tangible and empathetic approach.

4. Market Potential and Size

Identifying your target market is only half the journey. Assessing its potential size and growth helps in strategic planning. Utilize tools and databases like Statista, MarketResearch.com, or the US Census Bureau data to estimate market size.

5. The Evolving Nature of the Target Market

In the fluid world of consumer preferences, it's crucial to understand that target markets are not static. They evolve based on economic, social, technological, and individual changes. Regularly revisit your target market analysis to ensure continued relevance.

6. Pitfalls to Avoid

- **Over-generalization:** Casting the net too wide dilutes marketing efforts. It's crucial to be specific.

- **Assumptions:** Never base strategies on assumptions. Always validate with data.

- **Ignoring Niches:** Sometimes, the most loyal customer base comes from niche segments. Overlooking them could be detrimental.

7. Conclusion

In the sage words of *Maxwell Bridge*, "In the vast marketplace, pinpointing your target is the difference between a shot in the dark and a bullseye." Analyzing your target market, therefore, isn't just a preliminary step but a continuous process. It ensures that every effort, every strategy, and every message is tailored, resonant, and impactful. It turns the challenges of the vast marketplace into tangible opportunities. For, in the end, success in network marketing isn't about reaching everyone, but about deeply connecting with the right ones.

Selecting the Right Products or Services

The bedrock of any network marketing endeavor lies in its products or services. As **Maxwell Bridge** aptly states, *"Your product is the ship in which your network marketing journey sails. If it's not seaworthy, no amount of marketing will prevent it from sinking."* To thrive in this dynamic landscape, one must employ meticulous care in product selection, aligning with both market demand and personal convictions.

1. Understand Market Needs

Before diving into product selection, it's paramount to fathom the depths of market needs. A product that resonates with the current demands ensures not just initial traction but sustained growth.

- **Demand Analysis:** Use tools like Google Trends, market surveys, and industry reports to gauge product popularity and potential longevity in the market.

- **Gap Analysis:** Identify unmet needs in the market. These are opportunities for differentiation and can set you apart in a crowded marketplace.

2. Align with Personal Passion and Conviction

Network marketing is as much about the product as it is about personal stories. Promoting a product you genuinely believe in not only grants authenticity to your sales pitch but also makes the marketing journey more gratifying.

Tab. 17: Alignment Assessment

Criteria	Self-Assessment	Market Feedback
Passion for the product	(Rate on a scale of 1-10)	-
Product efficacy	-	(Collect user testimonials)
Sustainability	-	(Gauge long-term market interest)

3. Evaluate Product Quality and Efficacy

A product's success is tightly knit to its quality. In the age of reviews and testimonials, a subpar product can quickly spell the end of a promising network marketing career.

- **Test Before Promoting:** Always personally try the products. A first-hand experience grants credibility to your pitches and identifies potential strengths and weaknesses.

- **Solicit Feedback:** Gather reviews from other users. Understand the product's impact and any recurrent issues.

4. Consider Market Saturation

An oversaturated market can be challenging for newcomers. While established products have their credibility, breaking into a market teeming with similar offerings can be daunting.

- **Differentiation:** If entering a saturated market, ensure that the product has a unique selling point (USP) that sets it apart.

- **Niche Markets:** Sometimes, targeting a smaller segment with specific needs can lead to better results than broad markets.

5. Longevity vs. Trending Products

In network marketing, both evergreen products and trending products have their space. While evergreen products assure consistent demand, trending products can offer rapid growth.

- **Assess Product Lifecycle:** Understand where the product stands in its lifecycle. Is it a fleeting trend or here to stay?

- **Diversify:** A balanced portfolio of both types can offset the risks associated with each.

6. Training and Support

Products in network marketing often come with training and promotional materials. These resources can be pivotal, especially for newcomers.

- **Quality of Materials:** Ensure the product's company offers high-quality training, whether through seminars, webinars, or written guides.

- **Ongoing Support:** Companies that provide continuous updates and support reflect commitment to their distributors.

7. Ethical Considerations

Given the scrutiny network marketing often faces, ensuring that products adhere to the highest ethical standards is non-negotiable. This includes fair sourcing, eco-friendliness, and transparent business practices.

8. Pricing and Profit Margins

While passion for a product is vital, the economic viability cannot be sidelined. Understand the pricing structure, the potential return on investment, and how it compares to other products in the market.

9. Conclusion

In the eloquent words of **Maxwell Bridge**, *"Your product selection is a reflection of your business acumen, ethical stance, and personal brand."* As such, a deliberate, well-researched approach is non-negotiable. When the right product aligns with a well-crafted strategy, the amalgamation can become an unstoppable force in the realm of network marketing.

Leveraging Technology for Outreach

In the contemporary realm of network marketing, technology is not merely an accessory; it's a requisite. **Maxwell Bridge**, with his extensive tenure in the industry, affirms, *"The most profound shifts in network marketing successes in the past decade can be attributed, in no small part, to the astute leveraging of technology."* In an era characterized by digital transformation, a network marketer's prowess in harnessing technological tools can profoundly influence their outreach potential.

1. Understanding the Digital Terrain

Prior to delving into specific tools and strategies, a foundational comprehension of the digital landscape is imperative.

- **Digital Demographics:** Recognize where your target audience spends most of their time online. Whether it's social media, forums, or specific websites, identifying these platforms facilitates focused outreach.

- **Trend Analysis:** Utilize tools such as Google Analytics or SEMrush to discern online trends pertinent to your product or service.

2. Digital Tools for Enhanced Communication

The dawn of digitalization has democratized communication tools, many of which are indispensable for network marketers.

- **CRM Systems:** Platforms such as Salesforce or HubSpot can revolutionize relationship management, offering automation, analytics, and segmentation features.

- **Email Marketing Platforms:** Tools like Mailchimp or ConvertKit facilitate tailored email campaigns, segmenting audiences, and automating follow-ups.

- **Webinar and Video Conferencing:** Platforms like Zoom or WebEx are quintessential for hosting product demonstrations, training sessions, or team meetings.

Tab. 18: Key Digital Communication Tools

Tool Type	Recommended Platforms	Primary Benefits
CRM Systems	Salesforce, HubSpot	Automation, Analytics
Email Marketing	Mailchimp, ConvertKit	Segmentation, Automation
Video Conferencing	Zoom, WebEx	Virtual Demos, Training

3. Exploiting Social Media

In this digital epoch, overlooking social media is analogous to neglecting a goldmine of opportunities.

- **Platform Selection:** Not all social media platforms are created equal. Your product's nature and your target demographics should guide your platform choice—be it Instagram, LinkedIn, Twitter, or Facebook.

- **Content Strategy:** Regular posting of quality content, interspersed with product promotions, is essential. Use visual tools like Canva for creating engaging posts.

- **Engagement:** Beyond posting, engage with your audience through comments, polls, and direct messages.

4. The Power of Analytics

In the digital domain, actions generate data, and data, when wielded correctly, paves the path to optimization.

- **Website Analytics:** Tools such as Google Analytics shed light on website traffic, user behavior, and conversion funnels.

- **Social Media Insights:** Platforms like Facebook Insights and Instagram Analytics provide a deep dive into post performance, audience demographics, and optimal posting times.

5. Automation: Scaling Outreach Efforts

Automation, when executed judiciously, can amplify outreach efforts exponentially without proportionally increasing workload.

- **Marketing Automation Platforms:** Tools such as Marketo or ActiveCampaign can automate email campaigns, lead scoring, and even social media posts.

- **Chatbots:** Platforms like ManyChat can automate initial interactions on websites or social media, guiding potential leads through predefined funnels.

6. Leveraging Affiliate and Referral Platforms

Harnessing the power of the crowd, especially through technology, can amplify outreach efforts.

- **Affiliate Platforms:** Tools like ClickBank or ShareASale allow marketers to partner with affiliates, extending product reach.

- **Referral Software:** Platforms like ReferralCandy or Ambassador can streamline and incentivize the referral process, turning satisfied customers into active promoters.

7. Mobile Outreach

With an ever-increasing global populace accessing the internet via mobile devices, optimizing for mobile outreach is non-negotiable.

- **Responsive Design:** Ensure that all digital assets, especially websites, are mobile-responsive.

- **Mobile Apps:** Consider leveraging or even developing mobile applications if they offer tangible value to your product or service offering.

8. Continuous Learning and Adaptation

In the rapidly evolving world of technology, staying stagnant equates to moving backward.

- **Digital Training:** Regularly update your digital skill set. Platforms like Coursera or Udemy offer courses on everything from digital marketing to advanced analytics.

- **Stay Updated:** Subscribe to digital marketing blogs, attend webinars, and participate in forums to stay abreast of the latest trends and tools.

9. Conclusion

The intersection of network marketing and technology is rich with potential, yet fraught with challenges. As **Maxwell Bridge** succinctly encapsulates, *"In the digital age of network marketing, it's not the strongest who thrive, but those most responsive to change."* Embracing technology is not a mere strategic move but a foundational shift, one that can redefine the horizons of outreach and engagement in network marketing.

Building and Nurturing Relationships

In the intricate matrix of network marketing, where a myriad of strategies and tools beckon the marketer's attention, a singular truth remains inarguable: *relationships form the backbone of any successful network marketing endeavor.* As asserted by **Maxwell Bridge** in his varied experiences, "Network marketing transcends beyond mere sales or strategic outreach; at its heart, it's a relationship-centric endeavor." This chapter delves into the profound depth of relationship-building and nurturing, anchoring it as a cornerstone of authentic and sustainable network marketing success.

1. Recognizing the Paramountcy of Relationships

It's crucial, to begin with, an understanding of why relationships matter:

- **Trust Foundation:** In an industry often beset by skepticism, building trust through genuine relationships can be the differentiating factor.

- **Repeat Business:** A loyal customer, cultivated through relationship nurturing, is likely to repeatedly engage and even champion the product or service.

- **Referral Generation:** Satisfied and engaged individuals, grounded in trust, often become voluntary ambassadors, ushering in fresh leads without added effort.

2. The Anatomy of Relationship-Building in Network Marketing

Drawing from cognitive science and sociology, the structure of relationship-building can be viewed as a layered construct:

- **Acquaintance Stage:** Initial contact where impressions are formed. It is where rapport starts getting built.

- **Building Stage:** Where understanding deepens, trust gets fortified, and a mutual bond begins to form.

- **Consolidation Stage:** Deepened trust and mutual respect, often resulting in business transactions.

- **Nurturing Stage:** Continuous engagement, feedback loops, and further deepening of trust, leading to sustained business and referrals.

3. Strategies for Relationship Building

To effectively navigate the intricate relationship-building landscape, certain strategies can be instrumental:

- **Active Listening:** Listening, more than just hearing, to understand, empathize, and respond effectively.

- **Tailored Communication:** Understanding the unique preferences, pain points, and aspirations of each connection and customizing communication accordingly.

- **Transparency and Honesty:** Being open about the product, its benefits, and limitations. This cultivates trust and mitigates potential disillusionment.

- **Regular Check-ins:** Periodic, non-business-centric engagements to check on well-being or offer value without direct sales intent.

4. The Significance of Emotional Intelligence (EI)

Relationship-building is not a mechanistic process. **Emotional Intelligence**, the ability to understand, interpret, and manage one's own and others' emotions, plays a pivotal role:

- **Empathy:** The capacity to place oneself in another's shoes, crucial for trust-building.

- **Self-regulation:** Managing one's emotions, especially in challenging situations, to maintain relationship harmony.

- **Motivation:** Harnessing positive emotions to inspire and motivate, both oneself and others.

Tab. 19: Key Components of Emotional Intelligence

Components	Description	Application in Network Marketing
Self-awareness	Recognizing one's emotions and their impact.	Tailoring one's approach based on mood and state.
Self-regulation	Controlling and channeling one's emotions.	Managing rejections without bitterness.
Motivation	Being driven internally to achieve.	Inspiring prospects and team members.
Empathy	Recognizing and understanding the emotions of others.	Crafting tailored responses and solutions.
Social Skills	Managing relationships and building rapport.	Effective networking and team building.

5. The Role of Digital Platforms in Relationship Nurturing

In this digital age, maintaining a human touch while leveraging technology can be a game-changer:

- **Social Media Engagement:** Beyond posts and promotions, genuine engagement in comments, direct messages, and community groups.

- **Email Personalization:** Using tools to personalize email outreach, making the recipient feel valued and unique.

- **Virtual Meet-ups:** Hosting webinars, virtual coffee chats, or group discussions to maintain and deepen connections.

6. Managing Relationship Challenges

Even with the best intentions, challenges may arise:

- **Conflict Resolution:** Addressing misunderstandings promptly and constructively.

- **Feedback Acceptance:** Embracing critiques as avenues for growth and relationship deepening.

- **Re-engagement Strategies:** For dormant connections, innovative ways to reignite interest and engagement.

7. Conclusion

If network marketing is the vehicle driving one towards success, relationships undoubtedly are the fuel. As eloquently summarized by **Maxwell Bridge**, *"The edifice of network marketing, no matter how grand, rests precariously without the foundational bedrock of nurtured relationships."* Whether you're an industry neophyte or a seasoned expert, continuous investment in relationship-building and nurturing stands as the unequivocal pathway to sustained success in network marketing.

Chapter 6
Ethical Networking

Steering Clear of Pyramid Schemes and Scams

In a realm as dynamic and potent as network marketing, a lamentable shadow casts itself over eager entrepreneurs — the specter of pyramid schemes and scams. These unethical traps, though occasionally cloaked in the garb of legitimacy, can critically tarnish one's reputation, damage relationships, and lead to significant financial loss. Drawing from the fountain of wisdom that is **Maxwell Bridge's** extensive experience, this chapter aims to equip the reader with discernment tools and insights to sidestep these pitfalls.

1. Understanding the Subtleties

Before diving deep, it is paramount to demystify the terms and understand their inherent intricacies:

- **Pyramid Scheme:** A fraudulent investment scheme where returns for older investors are generated through the capital of newer ones. Notably, these schemes lack any genuine product or service offering and rely heavily on recruitment for revenue.

- **Scam:** A deceptive tactic or strategy to defraud an individual or organization. Within the context of network marketing, scams might involve counterfeit products, false advertising, or non-existent training programs.

2. The Allure of Pyramid Schemes

It's essential to comprehend why these schemes, despite their infamy, continue to lure individuals:

- **Promises of High Returns:** Offering seemingly incredible financial gains in a short span.

- **Aggressive Recruitment:** The primary focus remains on expanding the network rather than selling a genuine product or service.

- **Hyped Testimonials:** Cherry-picked success stories without a genuine representation of the average participant's experience.

3. Distinguishing Legitimate Network Marketing from Pyramid Schemes

Drawing a clear demarcation is vital. A few critical indicators include:

- **Genuine Product or Service:** Legitimate network marketing endeavors offer real value through their products or services.

- **Earnings Based on Sales:** Authentic operations reward based on product sales, not solely recruitment.

- **Transparent Business Model:** A genuine company will transparently share its revenue model, compensation plans, and other business specifics.

Tab. 20: Contrasting Pyramid Schemes & Legitimate Network Marketing

Aspect	Pyramid Scheme	Legitimate Network Marketing
Primary Revenue Source	Recruitment	Product/Service Sales
Financial Transparency	Opaque/Hidden	Transparent & Detailed
Training & Support	Focused on Recruitment	Comprehensive Product & Sales Training
Product/Service Value	Non-existent or of Low Value	High Quality & Competitive
Longevity	Short-lived (Collapses quickly)	Sustainable and Long-term

4. Navigating the Red Flags

While pyramid schemes and scams have evolved, some timeless red flags remain consistent:

- **Pressure to Invest:** High-pressure tactics, urging quick investment decisions without adequate contemplation.

- **Vague Business Model:** Lack of clarity on how the business genuinely generates revenue.

- **Unsubstantiated Earnings Claims:** Promises of extravagant incomes without any solid evidence.

5. Protective Measures

Forewarned is forearmed. Taking the following protective measures can safeguard against pitfalls:

- **Due Diligence:** Thoroughly researching a company, its leadership, business model, and product offerings.

- **Seeking External Counsel:** Consulting with industry experts, such as **Maxwell Bridge**, or seeking advice from unbiased third-party agencies.

- **Avoiding "Get Rich Quick" Lures:** Recognizing that genuine success in network marketing, as in any business, requires effort, time, and commitment.

6. Dealing with Entanglement in a Scheme

If one finds oneself inadvertently ensnared in a scheme, taking immediate remedial actions is crucial:

- **Disengagement:** Ceasing any further financial investments and disassociating from the scheme.

- **Legal Counsel:** Seeking legal advice, especially if substantial financial investments were made.

- **Sharing with the Network:** Informing one's network of the discovery, thus safeguarding them from potential harm.

7. Conclusion

In the ever-evolving realm of network marketing, the age-old adage remains pertinent — *if something seems too good to be true, it probably is.* With the nuanced insights provided by **Maxwell Bridge**, coupled with diligent research and discernment, one can navigate the expansive seas of network marketing, steering clear of the treacherous waters of pyramid schemes and scams. As with any journey worth undertaking, the path to authentic success in network marketing requires vigilance, dedication, and an unwavering commitment to ethical practices.

Authenticity vs. Manipulation

Network marketing, like any dynamic industry, presents practitioners with a myriad of strategic pathways, decisions, and ethical considerations.

None is more significant, perhaps, than the dichotomy between **authenticity** and **manipulation**. This critical juncture, when navigated with wisdom and integrity, can spell the difference between fleeting success and sustainable, respectable enterprise growth. Through the guidance of **Maxwell Bridge**, this chapter aims to delineate these two contrasting approaches, emphasizing the intrinsic value of authenticity and the pitfalls of manipulative tactics.

1. The Essence of Authenticity

Authenticity, as its etymology suggests, pertains to being genuine or of undisputed origin. Within the realm of network marketing, this translates to:

- **Transparent Intentions:** Engaging potential clients or recruits with sincerity and without ulterior motives.

- **Genuine Product Representation:** Presenting products or services honestly, without exaggeration or falsehoods.

- **Building Real Relationships:** Focusing on cultivating meaningful, lasting relationships over short-term transactional interactions.

2. The Machinations of Manipulation

Manipulation, on the other hand, is the act of skillfully or unfairly controlling or influencing a person or situation. In the context of network marketing, manipulative tactics can include:

- **False Promises:** Offering unrealistic benefits or results to entice recruits or customers.

- **Misrepresentation:** Deliberately misleading potential recruits or customers about the nature of the business, its prospects, or product effectiveness.

- **Pressure Tactics:** Employing psychological tricks or social pressure to induce someone to join or buy.

Tab. 21: Distinguishing Authenticity from Manipulation

Characteristics	Authenticity	Manipulation
Intent	Transparent & Sincere	Hidden & Self-serving
Product Presentation	Honest & Accurate	Exaggerated or False
Relationship Building	Long-term & Genuine	Short-term & Transactional

3. Ramifications of Choosing Manipulation Over Authenticity

The repercussions of manipulative tactics, though occasionally resulting in short-term gains, can have long-lasting negative impacts:

- **Damaged Reputation:** In an age of digital connectivity, disreputable actions can spread quickly, irreparably harming one's brand.

- **Loss of Trust:** Manipulation can erode trust, which is foundational in network marketing relationships.

- **Legal Repercussions:** Deceptive practices can lead to legal challenges or sanctions.

4. Benefits of Upholding Authenticity

Choosing authenticity isn't just an ethical choice; it's also a strategic one:

- **Sustained Growth:** Authentic businesses tend to have a longer, more sustainable trajectory.

- **Loyal Network:** Authenticity breeds trust, which in turn fosters loyalty among customers and recruits.

- **Positive Brand Image:** An authentic brand image is more likely to attract like-minded individuals and foster community.

5. Navigating the Gray Zones

While the distinction between authenticity and manipulation might appear black and white, real-world scenarios can present shades of gray. Thus, it's crucial to:

- **Stay Informed:** Regularly update one's knowledge about industry standards and best practices, ensuring alignment with the highest ethical standards.

- **Seek Feedback:** Periodically request feedback from peers, mentors, or industry veterans, such as **Maxwell Bridge**.

- **Reflect:** Regularly evaluate one's practices and intentions, ensuring alignment with core values and ethical standards.

6. Conclusion

The ethical crossroads of authenticity versus manipulation is one that every network marketer will face multiple times in their journey. However, as **Maxwell Bridge** so aptly demonstrates through his extensive experience, the path of authenticity, though occasionally challenging, is the one that not only honors the individual and the community but also paves the way for sustained success and respect in the industry.

Building Trust in an Often-Misunderstood Industry

Network marketing, despite its enduring history and proven success stories, remains an industry that is frequently misconstrued, leading to skepticism and doubt among many outsiders. However, one paramount tenet in navigating this industry, especially emphasized by **Maxwell Bridge** in his extensive practice, is the virtue of trust. Building trust, particularly in a realm that is so often misunderstood, is not a mere accessory to success but its very backbone. This chapter delves deep into understanding why trust is indispensable, the challenges in fostering it, and offers pragmatic steps towards engendering trust in network marketing.

1. The Indispensable Role of Trust

Trust functions as the linchpin in the world of network marketing. Without it:

- **Transactions Wane:** Purchases are not merely transactional; they're emblematic of trust between the marketer and the customer.

- **Recruitments Decline:** New members join not just because of an enticing product but because they trust the person introducing them to it.

- **Reputational Risk Amplifies:** Missteps are not just errors; they erode the fragile trust that's so hard to cultivate.

2. Factors That Undermine Trust in Network Marketing

To build trust, one must first understand the factors that commonly undermine it:

- **Misinformation:** Prevalent misconceptions about the industry lead many to erroneously equate all network marketing to pyramid schemes.

- **Past Scams:** High-profile scams have tarnished the image of legitimate businesses.

- **Inconsistent Messaging:** Marketers that lack a clear and consistent message can breed confusion and skepticism.

3. Building Trust: A Multi-faceted Approach

Trust, while intangible, is cultivated through consistent, tangible actions. Key strategies include:

- **Transparency:** Always be upfront about the business model, potential earnings, and the challenges ahead.

- **Consistency:** Ensure that the message you send about the products and the business remains unchanging.

- **Education:** Actively combat myths by educating potential recruits and clients about the genuine benefits and structure of network marketing.

Tab. 22: Trust Breakers vs. Trust Makers in Network Marketing

Aspects	Trust Breakers	Trust Makers
Information Sharing	Concealment & Ambiguity	Transparency & Clarity
Messaging	Inconsistency	Steadfast Consistency
Handling Misconceptions	Ignorance & Dismissal	Proactive Education & Engagement

4. Trust as a Continual Process

Trust isn't a one-time achievement; it's a continuous endeavor:

- **Continuous Engagement:** Regularly check in with your network, not just for business but to nurture relationships.

- **Feedback Mechanisms:** Create avenues for clients and recruits to share feedback, and importantly, act on it.

- **Ongoing Education:** As the industry evolves, ensure you're updating your network on latest practices, products, and strategies.

101

5. The Reciprocal Nature of Trust

In network marketing, trust isn't just a downward transaction from the marketer to the recruit or client. It's reciprocal:

- **Trust Your Products:** You can only build trust in others if you genuinely believe in the products you're promoting.

- **Trust Your Network:** Give them the tools and education they need, and trust them to use them wisely.

- **Trust Yourself:** As **Maxwell Bridge** emphasizes, believe in your capacity to navigate the challenges and nuances of the industry.

6. The Pivotal Role of Ethical Practices

The surest foundation of trust is an unwavering commitment to ethics:

- **Avoid Overpromising:** Always set realistic expectations.

- **Embrace Authenticity:** Opt for genuine narratives over embellished stories.

- **Prioritize Well-being:** The well-being of your recruits and clients should always supersede profit motives.

7. Conclusion

In the labyrinthine journey of network marketing, trust serves as the North Star. It guides actions, decisions, and strategies. Especially in an industry that's often clouded by misconceptions and skepticism, building and nurturing trust isn't optional—it's the lifeblood of success. Through the experienced lens of **Maxwell Bridge**, this chapter underscores not just the why, but the how of trust-building, providing network marketers an illuminating path in an industry that so often remains in shadows.

Chapter 7
Learning from Successes and Failures

Case Studies: What Went Right

In any industry, learning from real-world examples paves the way for a deeper understanding and nuanced approach to business. In network marketing, especially, these lessons become all the more crucial given the wide-ranging experiences and strategies that can either make or break an enterprise. By carefully examining successes, we not only celebrate victories but dissect the principles and practices that led to them. **Maxwell Bridge** emphasizes, through his unique vantage point, that case studies serve as tangible exemplars of principles previously discussed, giving substance to theory.

Note: Regarding the case studies highlighted below, we have used **fictitious names for the companies**, both for the negative and positive examples, in order to focus the reader **solely on the concepts expressed**. Here, the goal is to learn; we are not interested in gossip!

1. Network Marketing Enterprise: ProActive Solutions

Background: ProActive Solutions started as a small health and wellness MLM in 2015, focusing on organic supplements.

Keys to Success:

- **Diligent Market Research:** Before introducing any product, ProActive invested significant time in understanding market gaps.

- **Training & Development:** ProActive placed significant emphasis on continuous training, ensuring that their representatives were not only product experts but also skilled communicators.

- **Ethical Business Model:** Transparent income disclosures and a non-aggressive recruitment strategy built trust, both internally and externally.

Outcome: Within three years, ProActive Solutions expanded to 10 countries with over 50,000 active representatives.

2. Lifestyle and Beauty Brand: RadiantYou

Background: RadiantYou started its journey in the cosmetic realm with a singular focus on cruelty-free and sustainable products.

Keys to Success:

- **Distinct USP:** Their pledge against animal testing coupled with an eco-friendly approach carved a niche for them.

- **Leveraging Technology:** They incorporated AI-driven analytics to understand consumer behaviors, enabling tailored marketing strategies for different demographics.

- **Community Building:** Regular workshops, webinars, and retreats fostered a sense of belonging among the representatives.

Outcome: RadiantYou's turnover exceeded $100 million within five years, with a representative retention rate of over 80%.

Tab. 23: Comparative Success Metrics

Metrics	ProActive Solutions	RadiantYou
Years Active	3	5
Expansion (Countries)	10	8
Active Representatives	50,000	70,000
Turnover	Undisclosed	$100 million

3. Home & Living: SereneSpaces

Background: Capitalizing on the trend of home optimization, SereneSpaces focused on a range of eco-friendly home products.

Keys to Success:

- **Trend Utilization:** They astutely observed a growing trend towards sustainable living and promptly positioned their brand at its forefront.

- **Effective Branding:** A consistent branding message of 'eco-friendly luxury' was maintained across all touchpoints, from packaging to online platforms.

- **Collaborative Approach:** Encouraged collaborations among representatives for joint ventures and pop-up events, fostering community over competition.

Outcome: SereneSpaces was lauded for its business model by various industry experts and saw a 300% growth in sales over two years.

4. Personal Reflection by Maxwell Bridge

Maxwell Bridge interjects with a personal reflection here, accentuating that while the strategies differed among these case studies, the common underpinning was a genuine commitment to value provision, both to the customer and the representatives. He reiterates, "Success in network marketing isn't predicated solely on the 'network' or the 'marketing', but on the genuine value proposition, ethical grounding, and an unwavering commitment to continuous learning and adaptation."

5. Analytical Insights: Drawing the Threads Together

Drawing parallels among the aforementioned case studies:

- **Product Value and USP:** Each enterprise identified a niche or a trend, ensuring that their products or services filled a genuine market need.

- **Ethical Practices:** A transparent and ethical approach not only builds trust but fosters longevity in the network marketing realm.

- **Community-Centric Approach:** Emphasizing a sense of belonging, continuous learning, and collaboration over competition was pivotal.

6. Conclusion

Through these carefully curated case studies, the blueprint for success in network marketing becomes apparent. However, **Maxwell Bridge** emphasizes that while these success stories are enlightening, they should serve as inspiration rather than templates. Each network marketing journey is unique, dictated by its products, target audience, and the vision of its leaders. What remains universal, however, is the need for authenticity, value provision, and a genuine commitment to the growth and welfare of all stakeholders involved.

Case Studies: What Went Wrong

In the annals of network marketing, both success and failure hold critical lessons. The stories of failed endeavors not only provide cautionary tales but, more importantly, illuminate the pitfalls to avoid, the missteps that can lead to an endeavor's untimely demise. Under the guide of Maxwell Bridge's seasoned lens, we delve into these narratives, seeking wisdom in the misadventures of others.

Note: In these other case studies as well, we have used fictitious names for the companies to ensure the reader's focus remains on the didactic principles elucidated. The intention here is purely educational.

1. *AlphaNet Inc.* – Misunderstanding the Business Model

AlphaNet Inc. commenced operations with significant enthusiasm, attracting numerous participants with the allure of easy profits. However, their business strategy pivoted more towards recruitment than actual product sales. The result? A structure that bore an uncanny resemblance to a pyramid scheme.

Key Takeaway: It's paramount to understand that the essence of network marketing lies in product or service promotion. Recruitment should be a means to that end, not the primary revenue source.

2. *BrioConnect* – Over-reliance on a Single Strategy

While their health and wellness products were of commendable quality, *BrioConnect* relied almost entirely on in-person seminars for marketing. As digital trends became more pervasive, they were left behind, leading to dwindling sales and distributor engagement.

Key Takeaway: Flexibility and adaptability in strategies are pivotal. Over-reliance on a singular approach, especially in a dynamic industry, can be detrimental.

3. *TechnaSolutions* – Failing to Evolve with the Industry

TechnaSolutions ventured into the realm of tech-based network marketing. However, despite initial success, the company was resistant to technological advancements. Their refusal to integrate new digital tools and platforms caused inefficiencies, frustrating their network and customers alike.

Key Takeaway: Evolution is not a choice but a necessity. Embracing change and technological advancements ensures sustainability.

4. *PersonaCraft* – Neglecting Personal Development

This fashion-focused firm emphasized product knowledge, often at the expense of personal development. Distributors, although well-versed in product specifics, lacked essential soft skills, such as effective communication and empathy, leading to poor client relationships.

Key Takeaway: Product knowledge, while essential, must be complemented by personal growth and the development of soft skills.

5. *EduMark* – Underestimating Negative Stereotypes and Bias

Operating in the education sector, *EduMark* failed to address the prevalent skepticism surrounding network marketing. Without strategies to combat these stereotypes, potential clients often dismissed their offerings outright.

Key Takeaway: Addressing and rectifying biases is crucial. It's not enough to offer quality; companies must actively challenge and change negative perceptions.

Table 1.1: A Comparative Analysis of Missteps

Company	Primary Misstep	Secondary Effects
AlphaNet Inc.	Misunderstood Business Model	Decreased Trust, Legal Scrutiny
BrioConnect	Single Strategy Reliance	Decreased Engagement, Revenue Loss
TechnaSolutions	Resistance to Tech Evolution	Frustration, Operational Inefficiencies
PersonaCraft	Neglecting Personal Development	Poor Client Relationships
EduMark	Not Addressing Negative Stereotypes	Decreased Client Acquisition, Brand Reputation Damage

6. Conclusion

Failures, while often disheartening, serve as essential touchstones for growth and improvement. The companies highlighted above, encapsulating various sectors and strategies, all share a common thread - the neglection of foundational principles in network marketing. By studying these cautionary

112

tales, we can sidestep the common pitfalls and pave a smoother path towards network marketing success.

Remember, as Maxwell Bridge emphasizes throughout this tome, a holistic understanding, adaptability, and continuous learning are the cornerstones of enduring success in this industry.

Adapting and Innovating Based on Feedback

In a dynamic industry like network marketing, the ability to adapt and innovate based on feedback is not just beneficial—it's paramount to success. Maxwell Bridge's ten years of firsthand experience underscore this principle consistently: the most successful network marketers are those who view feedback as a goldmine for growth and innovation. The narrative that follows aims to elucidate the transformative power of feedback, presenting a methodology for its assimilation into strategies.

1. The Intrinsic Value of Feedback

Feedback, both positive and negative, carries with it an intrinsic value that can often be overlooked by novices in the industry. Positive feedback, while affirming, offers insights into the strengths of one's strategy—these are the elements to lean into and amplify. On the other hand, negative feedback, often dismissed or overlooked, holds within it the seeds for growth and refinement. By decoding the messages within these critiques, network marketers can recalibrate their strategies, ensuring alignment with market demands.

2. Feedback Channels and Their Utility

It's not just the feedback itself but also its sources that hold importance.

- **Direct Customer Feedback:** Engaging with end-users provides invaluable insights. These could come from product reviews, post-purchase surveys, or direct communications.

- **Peer Feedback:** Fellow network marketers, especially those outside your immediate circle, can offer a fresh perspective on strategies and approaches. Collaborative events, seminars, or informal meetups can be great platforms for this.

- **Digital Analytics:** In today's age, data reigns supreme. Tools like Google Analytics, social media insights, and CRM feedback loops offer real-time feedback on digital strategies. Metrics like customer engagement, bounce rate, and conversion ratios provide quantifiable measures to gauge effectiveness.

Tab. 24: Feedback Channels and Key Metrics

Channel	Key Metrics/Insights
Direct Customer Feedback	Product satisfaction, USP relevance
Peer Feedback	Strategy effectiveness, market trend alignment
Digital Analytics	Engagement rate, conversion ratio, website traffic

3. From Feedback to Action: A Structured Approach

Merely gathering feedback isn't enough; what truly matters is how it's leveraged. Maxwell Bridge suggests a structured approach:

1. **Collection:** Systematically collect feedback across channels. Employ tools and platforms to consolidate this information.

2. **Analysis:** Categorize feedback—Operational, Strategic, Tactical. Understand the root causes and not just superficial observations.

3. **Prioritization:** Not all feedback requires immediate action. Prioritize based on potential impact, feasibility, and alignment with long-term goals.

4. **Implementation:** Translate feedback into actionable steps. For example, if customers

115

indicate a preference for more eco-friendly packaging, explore sustainable options.

5. **Review:** After implementing changes, go back to the feedback loop. Assess if the actions taken have addressed the concerns or insights presented.

4. Avoiding Common Pitfalls

Adapting based on feedback is not without its challenges. Here are common pitfalls to avoid:

- **Overreaction:** Avoid making hasty changes based solely on a single piece of feedback. Look for patterns and consistency in feedback before making substantial shifts.

- **Confirmation Bias:** It's easy to gravitate towards feedback that confirms pre-existing beliefs. Challenge this by actively seeking diverse opinions.

- **Stagnation:** Do not let fear of negative feedback deter innovation. Constructive criticism is a stepping stone for growth, not a sign of failure.

5. Conclusion

In the tapestry of network marketing success, feedback threads are interwoven with resilience, adaptability, and innovation. By harnessing feedback effectively, network marketers can ensure that their strategies are not just in tune with current market dynamics, but are also poised to meet future challenges. After all, in Maxwell Bridge's own words, "In network marketing, adaptability is not just about survival; it's about thriving."

As we transition into the next chapter, remember: feedback is a compass, guiding your journey through the ever-evolving landscape of network marketing. Embrace it, learn from it, and let it chart your course to unparalleled success.

Chapter 8
Elevating Your Skill Set

Continuous Learning and Training Opportunities

In the realm of network marketing, the rapid pace at which the industry evolves necessitates a commitment to continuous learning and professional development. As Maxwell Bridge astutely emphasizes throughout his expansive tenure in the industry, "Stagnation in skill set is the Achilles' heel of the network marketer." In this chapter, the pivotal role of ongoing learning and the multifarious avenues for training are illuminated, reflecting Bridge's credence that knowledge acquisition is both the anchor and sail for navigating the turbulent seas of network marketing.

The Imperative of Lifelong Learning

Lifelong learning is not a mere choice but a critical imperative. The network marketing landscape is characterized by changing consumer behavior, technological advancements, and fluctuating market trends. To remain not just relevant but dominant, embracing continuous learning is quintessential.

- **Evolving Consumer Behavior:** As societal values and norms shift, so do the needs and wants of the consumer. Keeping abreast of these changes ensures the marketer's offerings remain pertinent.

- **Technological Advancements:** The digital age has revolutionized network marketing. Staying updated on the latest technological tools can provide a significant competitive edge.

- **Emerging Market Trends:** Identifying and understanding emerging trends can position a network marketer as a pioneer rather than a follower.

Opportunities for Continuous Learning

Network marketers are afforded a plethora of avenues for enhancing their skill set and knowledge base. A concise overview of the most efficacious channels is delineated below:

1. **Formal Education and Certification Programs:** Institutions now offer courses tailored specifically to network marketing. Whether online or in a classroom setting, these programs offer structured learning pathways, often culminating in recognized certification.

2. **Seminars and Workshops:** Industry leaders and experts frequently conduct seminars and workshops. These events provide real-time insights, hands-on training, and invaluable networking opportunities.

3. **Digital Courses and Webinars:** The rise of digital platforms like Coursera, Udemy, and LinkedIn Learning offers a vast reservoir of courses that can be accessed at one's convenience.

4. **Mentorship:** Building a relationship with a seasoned professional in the industry can provide personalized guidance, real-world insights, and nuanced strategies that generic courses might overlook.

5. **Industry Publications:** Regularly reading industry journals, magazines, and publications ensures one stays informed of the latest research, case studies, and trends.

Tab. 25: Learning Opportunities and Key Benefits

Opportunity	Key Benefits
Formal Education & Certification Programs	Structured learning, recognized certification
Seminars & Workshops	Real-time insights, hands-on training
Digital Courses & Webinars	Flexibility, vast array of topics
Mentorship	Personalized guidance, tacit knowledge transfer
Industry Publications	Updated research, industry trends

Tailoring Learning to Individual Needs

While the spectrum of learning opportunities is vast, it's paramount for network marketers to tailor their educational endeavors to their unique needs. Maxwell Bridge suggests a three-pronged approach:

1. **Self-Assessment:** Regularly evaluate your strengths and weaknesses. Understand where you excel and where there's room for growth.

2. **Feedback Loop:** Engage peers, mentors, and even competitors. Their feedback can provide an external perspective, revealing areas you might have overlooked.

3. **Customized Learning Path:** Based on the feedback and self-assessment, create a customized learning path. Prioritize areas that will have the most significant impact on your career trajectory.

The Tangible Impact of Continuous Learning

While the intrinsic value of knowledge is undeniable, in the world of network marketing, continuous learning has tangible benefits:

- **Increased Revenue Streams:** With more skills and knowledge, diversifying your product offerings or strategies can lead to new revenue streams.

- **Credibility & Authority:** Being knowledgeable positions you as an industry authority, garnering trust and respect from peers and customers alike.

- **Adaptability:** In an industry as volatile as network marketing, adaptability is crucial. Continuous learning ensures you remain agile, adapting to changes swiftly and effectively.

Conclusion

Maxwell Bridge's mantra, "In knowledge, there is power," reverberates throughout this chapter. Continuous learning is not just an added advantage; it is the lifeblood of a thriving network marketing career. In a world where change is the only constant, the commitment to ongoing education is the beacon that will guide network marketers through uncharted waters to the shores of unparalleled success. As you progress to the subsequent chapters, keep the sanctity of knowledge at the forefront of your mind, for it is the most potent tool in your arsenal.

Embracing Technology and Digital Tools

In the intricate realm of network marketing, success is not merely contingent on the products one sells or the relationships one nurtures, but significantly on how adeptly one adapts to the technological zeitgeist. As **Maxwell Bridge** has often posited, leveraging technology and digital tools is the linchpin to a transformative, efficacious network marketing strategy. This chapter delves deeply into the confluence of network marketing and digital technology, explicating the imperative of integrating the latter into the strategic tapestry of the former.

Digital Ascendance: The Changing Paradigm

In today's digitized era, the modus operandi of communication, commerce, and connectivity has transmuted substantially. Where face-to-face interactions once reigned supreme, digital channels now offer a parallel, if not predominant, avenue for engagement. The advent of this digital age is not just a fleeting trend but a paradigm shift, galvanizing industries, including network marketing, to adapt or risk obsolescence.

Significance of Digital Tools in Network Marketing

- **Pervasiveness of Outreach:** Digital platforms obliterate geographical constrictions, granting marketers an omnipresent reach. An adroitly crafted online campaign can reverberate across continents, transcending traditional locational barriers.

- **Precision Targeting:** Contemporary digital tools bequeath marketers with an unparalleled capability to target their audience with laser-like precision. Utilizing advanced algorithms and data analytics, it's feasible to reach an audience segment defined not just by age or location, but by nuanced interests, behaviors, and inclinations.

- **Instantaneous Feedback Loop:** The digital realm provides immediate feedback, be it through likes, shares, comments, or analytics. This feedback, both quantitative and qualitative, is instrumental for iterative refinement.

- **Scalability:** Digital strategies inherently possess the potential for scalability. A successful online campaign or system can be ramped up to cater to an exponentially larger audience with minimal incremental effort.

Choosing the Right Digital Arsenal

With a plethora of tools available, it's crucial to judiciously select ones that align with one's unique network marketing objectives and audience. Here is a schema that **Maxwell Bridge** proposes for classifying and understanding these tools:

Tab. 26: Categorization of Digital Tools

Type of Tool	Examples	Primary Utility
Content Management Systems	WordPress, Joomla	Creation and management of digital content, especially websites.
Social Media Platforms	Facebook, Instagram, LinkedIn	Branding, engagement, audience expansion, and feedback.
CRM Platforms	Salesforce, HubSpot	Managing customer interactions, data analytics, and follow-ups.
Email Marketing Solutions	Mailchimp, SendGrid	Direct engagement, personalized updates, and promotions.
Analytical Tools	Google Analytics, SEMrush	Traffic analysis, performance metrics, and audience insights.

Harnessing Digital Tools: A Guided Approach

1. Digital Audit: Begin by assessing your current digital footprint. Are you already using some tools? If yes, how effective are they in serving your goals?

2. Goal Definition: Clearly articulate what you wish to achieve with the digital tools. Is it brand visibility, lead generation, customer engagement, or all of the above?

3. Tool Selection: Based on the goals, choose tools that align closely with your needs. Remember, the most popular tool might not always be the most apt for your specific requirement.

4. Skill Acquisition: It's crucial to invest time in mastering the chosen tools. Whether it's a comprehensive CRM system or a social media platform, proficiency can markedly augment efficacy.

5. Continuous Iteration: The digital landscape is perpetually evolving. As such, periodic reviews and updates to your toolset and strategy are indispensable.

Potential Pitfalls and their Mitigation

Like every powerful weapon, digital tools, when misused, can backfire. Common pitfalls include overwhelming oneself with too many tools, neglecting data privacy regulations, and becoming overly reliant on automated processes at the cost of personal touch. To navigate these challenges:

- **Stay Updated:** Regularly update your knowledge about the tools you're using, ensuring compliance with any regulations and best practices.

- **Human Element:** While automation can augment efficiency, it's pivotal to maintain a personal touch, especially in a relationship-centric domain like network marketing.

- **Limit Tool Overload:** Avoid the allure of incessantly adding more tools to your arsenal. Instead, master a few that genuinely add value.

To encapsulate, as elucidated by **Maxwell Bridge**, embracing technology and digital tools is no longer a mere competitive advantage but an unequivocal necessity in the contemporary network marketing milieu. Integrating these tools into one's strategy, while being cognizant of potential pitfalls, can catalyze unparalleled success in the domain. As with all facets of network marketing, continuous learning, adaptation, and strategic vision are the keystones to leveraging the digital realm efficaciously.

Communication, Empathy, and Networking

In the intricate landscape of network marketing, where interpersonal dynamics underpin every transaction and relationship, soft skills emerge not just as beneficial, but unequivocally indispensable. While mastering the latest technologies or understanding market trends is undoubtedly important, a deep-seated proficiency in soft skills often determines the trajectory of one's success. Under the aegis of **Maxwell Bridge's** incisive insights, this chapter aims to dissect three foundational soft skills in the context of network marketing: Communication, Empathy, and Networking.

Communication: The Cornerstone of Network Marketing

At its core, network marketing is a business model built upon interpersonal interactions. Effective communication, therefore, transcends mere dialogue and delves into the realm of genuine understanding, active listening, and persuasive articulation.

- **Active Listening:** It's imperative to listen more than you speak. This means truly absorbing what the other party communicates, asking pertinent questions, and refraining from pre-emptive judgments. Active listening establishes trust and lays the foundation for long-term business relationships.

- **Clarity and Brevity:** In a world inundated with information, brevity is the soul not just of wit but of effective communication. Ensure your messages are clear, concise, and free from jargon, making them accessible to all.

- **Feedback Loops:** Effective communication is a two-way street. Creating avenues for feedback and genuinely acting upon it is vital for mutual understanding and growth.

Empathy: Connecting Beyond Business

In the words of **Maxwell Bridge**, "Network marketing, stripped of its commercial veneer, is fundamentally about human connections." Empathy, the ability to understand and share another's feelings and perspectives, is the linchpin of these connections.

- **Emotion over Transaction:** While sales and profits are tangible metrics of success, the intangible bonds forged through empathy often determine long-term success. Seeing beyond transactions to understand a client's aspirations, concerns, and motivations can deepen business relationships.

- **Empathy in Conflict Resolution:** Inevitably, misunderstandings and conflicts arise. Approaching such situations with empathy can de-escalate tensions and foster resolutions that strengthen, rather than strain, business ties.

- **Cultivating Empathy:** Empathy is not just an innate trait but a skill that can be honed. Regularly placing oneself in another's shoes, practicing active listening, and being genuinely curious about others are pathways to enhancing empathy.

Networking: Building Bridges Beyond Business

While the term "networking" inherently aligns with "network marketing," it's essential to understand its depth. Networking isn't about adding contacts but about cultivating meaningful, symbiotic relationships.

- **Quality over Quantity:** It's more fruitful to have a network of 10 deeply connected individuals than 100 superficial contacts. Foster depth in your connections.

- **Reciprocal Value:** True networking is reciprocal. While building your network, always ponder upon the value you can provide to others, rather than just what you can extract.

- **Networking Beyond Immediate Business Needs:** Engage with your network even when there isn't an immediate business need. Genuine check-ins, sharing relevant information, or just a simple greeting can sustain and deepen relationships.

Tab. 27: Soft Skills and Their Underlying Attributes

Soft Skill	Key Attributes
Communication	Active Listening, Clarity, Feedback Loops
Empathy	Emotional Understanding, Conflict Resolution, Continuous Cultivation
Networking	Depth of Connection, Reciprocal Value, Beyond-Business Engagement

In conclusion, while the technicalities of network marketing can be taught, it's the soft skills that often act as the differentiators between mediocrity and excellence. Through dedicated efforts, continuous self-awareness, and the judicious insights provided by veterans like **Maxwell Bridge**, one can elevate these skills, ensuring that they not only resonate in business transactions but transcend them, forging connections that last a lifetime.

Chapter 9
Turning the Ship Around: Practical Steps

Evaluating Your Current Status

"Without a thorough understanding of where you currently stand, the path to success remains obscured." - **Maxwell Bridge**

To orchestrate a transformative journey in network marketing, one must begin by taking a reflective pause to critically evaluate one's current status. This is not merely an act of self-awareness but a comprehensive process that digs deep into various facets of your network marketing enterprise. Embarking upon this introspective voyage, guided by the illuminating insights of **Maxwell Bridge**, we shall endeavor to dissect the nuances of this evaluation, making it both systematic and actionable.

1. Financial Assessment

Your financial metrics serve as a tangible reflection of your business health. Thus, a meticulous analysis is imperative.

- **Revenue Streams:** Analyze all sources of income. Identify which streams are most lucrative and which are underperforming.

- **Expenditure Breakdown:** Categorize and quantify all expenses. This helps in pinpointing unnecessary outflows and areas of potential cost-cutting.

- **Net Profit Margin:** This metric, obtained by deducting total expenses from total revenues, provides a clear picture of your actual earnings. It is the real litmus test of financial health.

2. Product Performance Analysis

Every product or service in your portfolio warrants scrutiny.

- **Sales Volume:** Which products are the most popular? Why?

- **Profit Margins:** High sales don't necessarily translate to high profits. Evaluate the profitability of each offering.

- **Customer Feedback:** Products that receive consistent negative feedback need reevaluation or possible discontinuation.

3. Relationship and Network Audit

In network marketing, relationships are the bedrock of success. Evaluating the quality and breadth of these relationships is crucial.

- **Active vs. Dormant Contacts:** Classify your contacts based on their recent engagement.

Devise strategies to rekindle dormant relationships.

- **Depth of Relationship:** Beyond numbers, assess the quality of each relationship. A few deep connections often outweigh numerous superficial ones.

- **Referral Analysis:** How many of your contacts actively refer you to others? A low referral rate might indicate trust issues or dissatisfaction.

4. Brand Perception and Digital Presence

In the digital age, your online brand image is a formidable determinant of success.

- **Online Engagement Metrics:** Utilize analytics tools to gauge website traffic, social media engagement, and online sales conversion rates.

- **Reputation Management:** Monitor online reviews, feedback, and mentions. Address negative reviews promptly and professionally.

- **Consistency Check:** Ensure that your brand messaging is consistent across all platforms, resonating with your core values.

5. Skills and Personal Development Review

Your personal growth invariably influences business growth in network marketing.

- **Training and Learning:** Have you kept abreast of industry trends, technologies, and strategies? Continuous learning is non-negotiable.

- **Soft Skills Assessment:** Revisit Chapter 8. How do you rate yourself in communication, empathy, and networking? Identify areas of improvement.

Tab. 28: Evaluation Metrics and Key Indicators

Evaluation Area	Key Indicators
Financial Assessment	Revenue Streams, Expenditure, Net Profit Margin
Product Performance	Sales Volume, Profit Margins, Customer Feedback
Relationship & Network	Active Contacts, Relationship Depth, Referral Rate
Brand & Digital Presence	Online Engagement, Reputation, Consistency
Skills & Personal Growth	Training, Soft Skills Assessment, Continuous Learning

In encapsulation, *evaluating your current status* is not a mere exercise in introspection but a rigorous, multifaceted analysis, aimed at achieving clarity. It is the foundational step in the grand edifice of network marketing success. Equipped with this clarity, a network marketer stands poised, not just to navigate the challenges but to reshape them into opportunities, all the while guided by the indomitable spirit and insights of **Maxwell Bridge**.

Setting Clear, Measurable Goals

"Vision without action is merely a dream. Action without vision just passes the time. Vision with action can change the world." - **Joel A. Barker**

Maxwell Bridge, in his rich tapestry of experiences, has often emphasized the axiom: *"Where clarity prevails, success ensues."* A vision, no matter how grand, if not translated into clear and measurable objectives, remains but a mere figment of one's imagination. In the nuanced world of network marketing, this principle takes on a heightened significance.

1. The Rationale Behind Clear Goals

Setting nebulous goals is akin to embarking on a voyage without a map. The journey becomes fraught with detours, confusions, and, more often than not, culminates in a dead end.

- **Focused Effort:** Clear goals act as beacons, guiding your actions and ensuring that your energies are directed towards meaningful endeavors.

136

- **Resource Allocation:** With precise goals, you can allocate resources, both tangible and intangible, in an optimized manner, ensuring minimal wastage.

- **Motivation and Morale:** Clearly defined objectives serve as milestones. Achieving these boosts confidence and morale, providing the impetus to tackle bigger challenges.

2. Characteristics of Measurable Goals

The concept of measurability ensures that you're not merely shooting in the dark. Instead, you have a quantifiable metric against which progress can be benchmarked.

- **Quantifiable:** Every goal must have a number. Whether it's revenue, customers, or engagement rates, having a numeric target ensures clarity.

- **Time-bound:** Assign a deadline. This creates urgency and fosters a sense of responsibility.

- **Realistic:** While it's important to aim high, goals should be set in the realm of possibility. Unrealistic targets often lead to demotivation.

- **Relevant:** Each goal should align with your overarching vision and strategy, ensuring cohesion in action.

3. The SMART Framework

One of the widely accepted methodologies for goal setting is the **SMART** framework. Grounded in pragmatism and simplicity, it encapsulates the essence of effective goal creation.

Tab. 29: The SMART Framework Explained

Element	Description
S	Specific - Goals should be clear and concise.
M	Measurable - Each goal must have criteria for measuring progress.
A	Achievable - It should be attainable given the current resources and constraints.
R	Relevant - The goal must align with the broader objectives and vision of the network marketing endeavor.
T	Time-bound - A clear deadline ensures focus and prioritization.

4. Periodic Review and Calibration

Even the most meticulously set goals require periodic introspection. The dynamic landscape of network marketing necessitates flexibility and adaptability.

- **Regular Monitoring:** Keep a tab on the progress at regular intervals. This ensures timely course corrections.

- **Feedback Mechanism:** Create a system where feedback, both internal (from team members) and external (from clients and partners), is sought, evaluated, and integrated.

- **Calibration:** Based on feedback and the changing external environment, recalibrate goals, ensuring they remain relevant and achievable.

5. The Psychological Dimensions

Goals are not just objective targets. They have profound psychological implications.

- **Commitment:** When you set a goal, it's a commitment to yourself. It's a declaration of intent, a pact that needs to be honored.

- **Visualization:** Visualize achieving your goals. This mental image serves as a powerful motivator, pushing you towards realization.

- **Emotional Resonance:** Your goals should resonate emotionally. They should not just be a business objective but something that you are passionate about.

In conclusion, the act of setting clear, measurable goals is both an art and a science. It demands introspection, understanding, and a profound grasp of the intricacies of the network marketing realm. It's an endeavor that goes beyond mere numbers, resonating deeply with the psyche, galvanizing one towards transformative actions. Guided by the insights of **Maxwell Bridge**, this chapter is not just a guide to setting goals but a testament to the transformative power of clarity and precision in intent. Let these principles be the foundation upon which you construct your edifice of success in network marketing.

Implementing Changes Step-by-Step

"A journey of a thousand miles begins with a single step." - **Lao Tzu**

Given the multifaceted and dynamic landscape of network marketing, Maxwell Bridge frequently advocates for an iterative, step-by-step approach to enacting change. Much like any intricate process, diving headfirst without a systematic game plan often results in missed opportunities, wasted resources, and scattered energies.

1. The Need for a Step-by-Step Approach

Complex processes demand a systematic methodology. To bring about a substantive change, particularly in a realm as nuanced as network marketing, demands a measured, progressive strategy.

- **Mitigating Risks:** Systematic implementation curtails risks by allowing for periodic evaluations, ensuring misguided steps can be corrected promptly.

- **Resource Management:** A phased approach ensures optimized use of resources, be it capital, human efforts, or time.

- **Feedback Integration:** By enacting changes iteratively, feedback can be garnered and incorporated in real-time, refining subsequent steps.

2. The Blueprint for Implementation

The guiding principle in step-by-step implementation lies in the harmonious blend of foresight, adaptability, and meticulous planning.

a. Assess the Current State

Before charting the course ahead, one must first have a lucid understanding of where they stand.

- **SWOT Analysis:** Conduct a comprehensive **SWOT (Strengths, Weaknesses, Opportunities, Threats)** assessment. This provides a clear picture of the internal and external factors influencing your network marketing endeavors.

141

- **Feedback Collection:** Garner feedback from peers, subordinates, clients, and other stakeholders. These insights offer a grassroots-level perspective, often highlighting overlooked aspects.

b. Prioritize the Changes

Once the landscape is clear, the next step is prioritization.

- **Impact vs. Effort Matrix:** Plot the changes on an 'Impact vs. Effort' graph. This helps in identifying changes that offer the most significant benefits for the least effort, ensuring quick wins.

Tab. 30: Impact vs. Effort Matrix

	High Effort	Low Effort
High Impact	Strategic Initiatives	Quick Wins
Low Impact	Low Priority	Minimal Benefits

c. Develop an Action Plan

With priorities set, draft a detailed action plan.

- **Set Clear Milestones:** Break down the change process into specific milestones, each with its defined set of deliverables.

- **Allocate Resources:** Based on the nature and scale of each milestone, allocate necessary resources, ensuring every phase is well-equipped for success.

- **Establish a Timeline:** Every milestone should have a clearly defined start and end date, fostering a sense of urgency and commitment.

d. Execute with Precision

The planning phase is followed by rigorous execution.

- **Stay Committed:** Changes, especially transformative ones, can be challenging. It's imperative to remain unwaveringly committed to the set course.

- **Monitor Progress:** Keep a keen eye on the progress. Use Key Performance Indicators (KPIs) to ensure that milestones are being achieved as per the set standards.

- **Iterative Feedback:** As changes are implemented, continuously seek feedback, ensuring that the implementation remains aligned with the desired objectives.

e. Review and Refine

Post-implementation, indulge in a thorough review.

- **Measure Against KPIs:** Assess the outcome against the pre-defined KPIs to gauge the success of the implementation.

- **Feedback Loop:** Revisit the feedback collected during the execution phase. Understand what went right and where there were lapses.

- **Refinement:** Based on the feedback and the outcome assessment, refine the strategy for future implementations.

In essence, implementing changes, particularly in a domain as intricate as network marketing, is not a sprint but a marathon. It requires patience, diligence, and the sagacity to understand that every step, no matter how small, is a stride towards the larger goal. Maxwell Bridge's insights, carved from a decade of experience, resonate with the timeless wisdom that in systematic progression lies the key to transformative success. Let this chapter serve as a testament to the power of phased, iterative change, guiding you towards the zenith of your network marketing endeavors.

Monitoring Progress and Adjusting as Needed

In the dynamic and ever-evolving realm of network marketing, *it is not enough to merely set the ship's course; one must also continuously ensure that the vessel is on track.* Maxwell Bridge, with his decade-long expertise, underscores the significance of continuous monitoring and course correction. As the famous adage by Peter Drucker goes, "What gets measured, gets managed." This chapter delves deep into the intricacies of how one should systematically monitor progress and adjust strategies in real-time, ensuring a trajectory towards success.

1. The Imperative of Continuous Monitoring

Before diving into the specifics, one must first understand the non-negotiable need for persistent monitoring.

- **Stay Ahead of the Curve:** Continuous monitoring allows one to spot emerging trends, new challenges, and potential threats, equipping them to take preemptive actions.

- **Efficiency and Optimization:** It helps in identifying inefficiencies, bottlenecks, and underperforming strategies, thereby guiding resource reallocation.

- **Stakeholder Confidence:** Demonstrated oversight and a proactive approach enhance trust among stakeholders, be they customers, peers, or subordinates.

2. Tools and Techniques for Effective Monitoring

Given the multifarious nature of network marketing endeavors, an amalgamation of tools and techniques is required for a comprehensive oversight.

- **Key Performance Indicators (KPIs):** These are quantifiable measures used to evaluate the success of an activity. Examples include customer acquisition rate, retention rate, and sales conversion ratio.

- **Dashboards:** Digital dashboards provide a real-time overview of multiple metrics, presenting a holistic snapshot of ongoing activities.

- **Feedback Loops:** Regularly solicit feedback from both internal teams and external clients. This offers qualitative insights complementing the quantitative metrics.

- **Competitor Benchmarking:** Regularly assess how your progress stands relative to your competitors. This helps in spotting gaps and understanding industry standards.

Tab. 31: Suggested KPIs for Network Marketing

KPI Category	Metric
Engagement	Social Media Engagement Rate
Acquisition	New Customer Acquisition Rate
Retention	Customer Retention Percentage
Sales	Average Sales per Representative
Feedback	Customer Satisfaction Score

3. Adjusting Strategies: The Art of Pivoting

No matter how impeccable a strategy might seem at the outset, the dynamic nature of the market often demands adjustments. This is where the real mastery lies - in the ability to pivot effectively.

- **Identify the Need:** Regular monitoring will throw up red flags. Recognizing these early is key. Whether it's a plummeting KPI or consistent negative feedback, be alert to these signs.

- **Root Cause Analysis:** Before any course correction, understand the underlying issues. Delve deep to pinpoint whether it's a market trend, internal inefficiency, or a broader industry shift.

- **Iterative Testing:** Instead of a complete strategy overhaul, try tweaking specific

147

elements and then testing. This could be a new marketing channel, a different sales script, or a modified product offering.

- **Incorporate Feedback:** Use the feedback, both from internal teams and external clients, to refine strategies. Feedback is a goldmine that offers direct insights into where adjustments might be needed.

- **Seek Expert Insights:** Sometimes, internal teams might be too close to the problem to see it. In such cases, seeking external expertise or a consultant's perspective can be invaluable.

4. Balancing Persistence with Flexibility

Maxwell Bridge, in his seasoned wisdom, emphasizes the delicate equilibrium between persistence and flexibility. While it's vital to be agile and adapt, it's equally crucial not to abandon strategies prematurely. Often, patience and perseverance are as essential as the willingness to change.

In conclusion, *navigating the seas of network marketing is not a static endeavor.* It demands vigilance, agility, and a meticulous blend of planning and adaptability. By systematically monitoring progress and adjusting as needed, network marketers can ensure that they not only stay afloat but sail with prowess, always adjusting their sails to catch the winds of opportunity. This proactive approach, distilled from Maxwell Bridge's decade of hands-on experience, stands as a cornerstone for anyone aspiring to turn their network marketing fortunes around.

Chapter 10
Sustaining Success

Building a Loyal Customer Base

In network marketing, while the initiation of a new customer connection is a laudable feat, the true hallmark of sustainable success lies in fostering an unbreakable bond of loyalty. A study by Bain & Company highlighted that increasing customer retention rates by 5% increases profits by 25% to 95%. This alone underscores the financial imperative of nurturing a steadfast clientele. In the encapsulated wisdom of Maxwell Bridge, *it's not the initial sale, but the subsequent bond that truly defines profitability.*

1. Understanding Customer Loyalty in Network Marketing

At its core, customer loyalty is not merely repetitive purchasing behavior but a genuine preference for a brand or representative, even in the face of alternatives.

- **Emotional vs. Transactional Loyalty:** While transactional loyalty is driven by the logic of deals or rewards, emotional loyalty is anchored in trust, rapport, and genuine satisfaction. In the long run, emotional loyalty proves to be far more sustainable.

- **The Loyalty Lifecycle:** Customers evolve from being prospects to first-time buyers, repeat customers, loyal clients, and finally brand advocates. The zenith of loyalty is when they become evangelists, voluntarily promoting and referring your offerings.

2. The Pillars of Building Loyalty

Building loyalty isn't an overnight endeavor. It's a meticulous cultivation of several key pillars.

- **Trustworthiness:** In the oft-misunderstood landscape of network marketing, trust is paramount. Honesty, transparency, and consistency are the cornerstones here.

- **Value Proposition:** Beyond the product or service, it's the added value you bring – be it through expert advice, personalized recommendations, or genuine care for client needs.

- **Engagement:** Regular interactions, be it through newsletters, social media, or personal check-ins, keep you on top of the client's mind.

- **Recognition and Rewards:** Recognizing milestones, celebrating anniversaries, or even simple gestures like birthday wishes can go a long way.

3. Avoiding Detractors of Loyalty

As Maxwell Bridge astutely points out, while there are strategies to build loyalty, it's equally critical to avoid pitfalls that can erode it.

- **Over-promising and Under-delivering:** Ensure that expectations set during the selling process are met post-sale. A mismatch can quickly erode trust.

- **Inconsistency:** Whether in product quality, service, or communication, inconsistency can bewilder and alienate customers.

- **Neglect:** Taking existing customers for granted and not investing in post-sale relationship-building can be a fatal error.

4. Metrics to Measure Customer Loyalty

To ensure that your strategies are effective, consistent measurement is imperative.

- **Net Promoter Score (NPS):** A simple metric that gauges the likelihood of a customer recommending your product or service to others.

- **Customer Retention Rate:** The percentage of customers who continue to buy over a specific time frame.

- **Customer Lifetime Value (CLV):** A measure of the net profit attributed to the entire future relationship with a customer.

Tab. 32: Key Loyalty Metrics and Their Significance

Metric	Significance
NPS	Gauges overall customer satisfaction and loyalty
Retention Rate	Assesses longevity of customer relationships
CLV	Predicts the total value of a customer over time

5. Leveraging Technology for Loyalty Building

In today's digital age, technology offers myriad tools to automate, enhance, and refine loyalty-building.

- **Customer Relationship Management (CRM) Systems:** These tools allow for personalized customer interactions, ensuring every client feels unique and valued.

- **Automated Reward Systems:** Automate the process of recognizing and rewarding customers, ensuring no milestone goes unnoticed.

- **Feedback Platforms:** Digital platforms that collate customer feedback can provide invaluable insights into areas of improvement.

In the words of Maxwell Bridge, *"Loyalty is the lifeblood of network marketing."* While the initial acquisition of a customer is a test of your selling prowess, the retention and cultivation of that relationship is a testament to your character, value proposition, and genuine commitment to the client's well-being. Building a loyal customer base, thus, is not just a strategy for profitability, but a reflection of your ethos as a network marketer. And in this realm, with the right strategies and the heart in the right place, the sky's the limit.

Diversifying Revenue Streams

The adage, *"Don't put all your eggs in one basket,"* has long been used to underline the dangers of a single-source dependency for income. For network marketers, especially in the ever-fluctuating arena we operate in, this wisdom is not just advice—it's imperative. Diversifying revenue streams, in essence, is about creating multiple avenues of income to mitigate risks associated with any one of those channels underperforming. Maxwell Bridge's journey, stretching over a decade, showcases a tapestry of multiple revenue streams that have served as both a safety net and a catapult for growth.

1. The Conceptual Framework of Revenue Diversification

Before delving into strategies, it's crucial to grasp the 'why' behind diversification.

- **Risk Mitigation:** The primary benefit of diversification is risk dispersion. If one stream falters, others can compensate, ensuring steady overall revenue.

- **Optimizing Opportunities:** Different streams can peak at different times, ensuring a more consistent income flow.

- **Capitalizing on Strengths:** Diversifying allows marketers to leverage their myriad skills, from direct selling to digital marketing.

2. The Anatomy of Revenue Diversification in Network Marketing

In the network marketing sphere, diversifying goes beyond selling different products.

- **Product Diversification:** Offering a range of products caters to a broader segment of the target market. However, ensure products align with your brand and expertise.

- **Digital Products and Courses:** Your expertise is valuable. Create digital courses, webinars, or e-books to teach others the nuances of network marketing.

- **Affiliate Marketing:** Partner with brands or services resonating with your audience. Promote their offerings for a commission on sales.

- **Consultation and Mentorship:** Leverage your experience to offer consultancy services to budding network marketers.

- **Investments:** Use a portion of your earnings to invest in stocks, bonds, or real estate. These passive income sources can offer stability.

Tab. 33: Different Revenue Streams and Their Viability

Revenue Stream	Pros	Cons
Product Diversification	Access to varied market segments	Requires extensive product knowledge
Digital Products	Scalable; Passive income	Initial time investment; Need for regular updates
Affiliate Marketing	Less inventory management; Extra income	Dependence on third-party brands
Consultation	Capitalizes on expertise; High-value service	Time-intensive; Requires established credibility
Investments	Passive income; Potential high returns	Requires financial acumen; Market risks

3. Strategies for Successful Revenue Diversification

- **Research and Knowledge:** Before venturing into a new stream, conduct thorough market research. Understand the demand, competition, and potential ROI.

- **Maintain Brand Consistency:** Every new venture should resonate with your core brand values and message. Dissonance can alienate your clientele.

- **Continuous Learning:** Regularly update your skills and knowledge to stay relevant in every stream you're involved in.

- **Financial Management:** Regularly assess the profitability of each stream. Allocate resources optimally and be ready to pivot if one stream starts underperforming.

4. The Caveats of Diversification

While diversification has its merits, Maxwell Bridge emphasizes the potential pitfalls:

- **Overextension:** Venturing into too many streams simultaneously can dilute your focus and reduce overall efficacy.

- **Inconsistency:** Different streams require varied strategies. Inconsistency in approach can hinder success in any given avenue.

- **Diminished Quality:** Spreading yourself too thin might affect the quality of service or product you offer.

Conclusion

In the vast ocean of network marketing, diversifying revenue streams is like having multiple sails. While one might falter in the absence of wind, others can catch the breeze, ensuring you keep moving forward. However, while diversification is a potent strategy, it demands judicious application. In the wise words of Maxwell Bridge, *"Diversification is not just about multiplying revenue avenues but about optimally allocating your time, energy, and resources to ensure each stream is a gushing source of income and not a mere trickle."*

Investing in Personal and Professional Growth

The realm of network marketing, as Maxwell Bridge eloquently illustrates through his decade-long voyage, is one of perpetual motion. Not only does the landscape evolve, but the tools, strategies, and the intrinsic value of personal growth within it also undergo metamorphosis. When one addresses the paradigm of 'growth' within this industry, it isn't merely the ascendancy of revenue, but the holistic enhancement of the individual at its helm. A network marketer's most invaluable asset isn't the products

158

they sell but the evolving repository of knowledge, skills, and personal attributes they bring to the table. This chapter delves into the profound significance and mechanisms of investing in personal and professional growth.

1. Understanding the Interplay of Personal and Professional Growth

It's pivotal to discern that personal and professional growth, though distinct in their trajectories, are inextricably intertwined.

- **Personal Growth:** This pertains to the evolution of an individual's character, emotional intelligence, resilience, and broader life skills.

- **Professional Growth:** Focused on the acquisition of skills, knowledge, and competencies directly related to the network marketing profession.

Both these realms influence and bolster each other. An enhancement in emotional intelligence (personal) can significantly amplify sales negotiation outcomes (professional), for instance.

2. The Pillars of Personal Growth in Network Marketing

- **Self-awareness:** Understand your strengths, weaknesses, aspirations, and fears. This clarity can be the compass directing your growth endeavors.

- **Emotional Resilience:** In an industry rife with rejections and setbacks, cultivating emotional fortitude is crucial. It ensures that challenges become stepping stones, not stumbling blocks.

- **Lifelong Learning:** Adopting the mindset of a perpetual student ensures adaptability and relevance in an evolving world.

Tab. 34: Components of Personal Growth and Their Relevance

Component	Relevance to Network Marketing
Self-awareness	Tailoring strategies based on innate strengths; Recognizing areas for training
Emotional Resilience	Navigating rejections and setbacks with grace; Maintaining motivation
Lifelong Learning	Staying updated with industry trends; Evolving with the market dynamics

3. The Cornerstones of Professional Growth

- **Skill Augmentation:** Regularly enrolling in courses or workshops to update your skills, be it sales techniques, digital marketing, or understanding consumer psychology.

160

- **Networking:** Building relationships with other professionals provides insights, opens opportunities, and fosters collaborative growth.

- **Feedback Integration:** Regularly seek feedback from peers, mentors, and customers. Constructive criticism is a goldmine for improvement.

4. Mechanisms for Facilitating Growth

- **Mentorship:** Aligning with industry veterans like Maxwell Bridge can offer tailored guidance, providing shortcuts to success.

- **Continued Education:** Enroll in formal courses, attend seminars, or indulge in self-paced online modules. The world is replete with knowledge; it's about reaching out and grasping it.

- **Reflective Practices:** Journaling, meditation, and introspective exercises can significantly enhance self-awareness and directionality in growth endeavors.

5. Monitoring and Evaluating Growth

It's not sufficient to just invest in growth; one must have metrics and mechanisms to evaluate it.

- **Setting Clear Benchmarks:** Whether it's mastering a new sales technique or enhancing emotional intelligence, have clear, measurable goals.

- **Regular Reviews:** Periodically assess where you stand vis-à-vis your benchmarks. This not only gauges progress but also provides direction for future endeavors.

6. The Symbiotic Relationship of Growth and Success

As Maxwell Bridge's illustrious career demonstrates, success in network marketing is a direct byproduct of relentless personal and professional evolution. Every step taken towards growth—be it reading a book, attending a seminar, or practicing mindfulness—translates to enhanced efficacy in the network marketing domain.

Conclusion

Investing in personal and professional growth isn't just a luxury or a side endeavor—it's the lifeblood of sustainable success in network marketing. As the landscape evolves, so must the network marketer. Each day presents a new opportunity, a fresh challenge, and an uncharted territory of growth. Maxwell Bridge's journey underscores a salient truth: *In the world of network marketing, growth isn't just about scaling revenue or expanding networks; it's about the ceaseless evolution of the soul behind the success.* Embrace growth, for it's the wind beneath the wings of your network marketing aspirations.

Conclusion

The Ever-Evolving Journey of Network Marketing

In the vast expanse of entrepreneurial endeavors, few industries have witnessed such a dynamic transformation as network marketing. Drawing parallels from the illustrious journey of Maxwell Bridge, one quickly discerns that this transformation is not merely an external phenomenon, but an intricate interplay of internal evolutions, external market forces, and the relentless march of technology. In this chapter, we will embark on an expedition, tracing the labyrinthine pathways of network marketing's evolution, drawing from its rich history and projecting into its promising future.

1. A Retrospective Glimpse

To appreciate the present, we must honor the past. Network marketing, in its nascent stages, was an embodiment of direct sales, characterized by face-to-face interactions, product demonstrations, and primarily relationship-based marketing.

Tab. 35: Timeline of Network Marketing Evolution

Era	Characteristics
The Foundational Years (Pre-1980s)	Face-to-face selling, reliance on close-knit community networks, localized operations
Expansion Era (1980s-1990s)	Advent of global expansion, development of structured training programs, increasing skepticism & regulatory scrutiny
Digital Dawn (2000s-2010s)	Integration of online tools, rise of social media as a marketing platform, diversification of product offerings
Contemporary Phase (2020s and Beyond)	Hybrid marketing strategies, AI-driven personalized outreach, emphasis on ethical practices, rise of community-centric models

2. The External Catalysts

Like every industry, external forces have significantly sculpted the contours of network marketing.

- **Technological Proliferation:** The digital era opened floodgates, allowing marketers to reach a global audience, utilize data-driven strategies, and achieve unprecedented scales of personalization.

- **Regulatory Frameworks:** As the industry expanded, it beckoned the eyes of regulators, ensuring that ethical practices were adhered to and setting clear demarcations between genuine network marketing and pyramid schemes.

- **Globalization:** With barriers diminishing, network marketing morphed from a local phenomenon to a global enterprise, replete with its challenges and opportunities.

3. The Internal Metamorphosis

Inwardly, the industry witnessed a seismic shift in paradigms, attitudes, and methodologies.

- **From Sales to Relationships:** No longer was the focus solely on selling products. Building lasting relationships became paramount, fostering trust and creating lifelong customers.

- **Holistic Development:** As Maxwell Bridge's biography exemplifies, the emphasis shifted from mere sales techniques to a holistic development of the marketer, encompassing personal growth, resilience, and adaptability.

- **Ethical Reinforcement:** With increased scrutiny and a more informed customer base, the importance of ethics and authenticity rose to the forefront.

4. Preparing for the Future: Trends to Watch

- **Community-centric Models:** The future is poised to be less about individual selling and more about building and nurturing communities that believe in the product's value.

- **AI and Big Data:** Tailoring strategies based on predictive analytics and personalized algorithms will become the norm rather than the exception.

- **Sustainability and Social Responsibility:** Modern customers are discerning, seeking not just quality products but ethical and sustainable business practices.

5. The Lessons Embedded in Evolution

The undulating journey of network marketing teaches resilience, adaptability, and the importance of staying attuned to external and internal shifts. But perhaps, most poignantly, it underscores a truth, echoed in Maxwell Bridge's journey — that success in this realm is not about resisting change, but dancing with it, harmoniously and adeptly.

Final Musings

The narrative of network marketing is far from complete. It's a tome that continues to be written with each passing moment, each sale made, and each relationship forged. Drawing from the wisdom embedded in its history, equipped with modern tools and insights, and fueled by the passion and commitment of network marketers like Maxwell Bridge, the journey promises to be one of continued growth, transformation, and unprecedented success.

In the words of Maxwell Bridge, *"Network marketing, much like life, is not a static experience but a dynamic journey. Embrace its ebb and flow, and therein lies the secret to unparalleled success."* This book, therefore, stands not as a mere retrospective account but as a clarion call to embrace the future, with all its uncertainties, challenges, and boundless opportunities.

Your Roadmap to Success: Commitment, Adaptation, and Persistence

In the vast and intricate landscape of network marketing, individuals embark on a journey paved with challenges and opportunities. Amid the numerous strategies, tactics, and methodologies that they encounter, three core tenets emerge as guiding beacons, illuminating the path to success: **Commitment, Adaptation, and Persistence**.

Drawing from the wisdom of Maxwell Bridge, the path to mastering network marketing isn't one of mere strategies or superficial techniques, but a deeply personal journey of cultivating these foundational attributes.

1. Commitment: The Bedrock of Your Endeavors

- **Defining Commitment:** At its core, commitment in the realm of network marketing signifies an unwavering dedication to your vision, goals, and the community you aim to serve. It's not a fleeting surge of motivation but a consistent, burning drive.

- **Commitment in Practice:** This entails immersing oneself in the intricacies of the industry, dedicating time to continuous learning, and upholding the ethics and values integral to genuine network marketing practices.

- **Measuring Commitment:** A committed marketer will not measure success solely by immediate sales or profits, but by deeper metrics such as client relationship quality, brand integrity, and personal growth.

Tab. 36: Commitment Milestones in Network Marketing

Aspect	Milestones
Learning	Regular upskilling, attending industry seminars, embracing new tools and technologies
Relationship Building	Regular follow-ups, creating value for clients, seeking feedback
Ethical Practices	Transparent communication, avoiding hard-sell tactics, prioritizing customer needs over quick sales

2. Adaptation: The Ability to Dance with Change

- **Embracing Fluidity:** As detailed in previous chapters, network marketing has witnessed numerous evolutionary phases. Adaptation isn't about mere reaction but proactive engagement with change.

- **Learning from the Landscape:** Network marketing, like any dynamic field, presents trends, shifts, and patterns. Adapting involves discerning these patterns, understanding their implications, and molding one's approach accordingly.

- **Technological Adaptation:** The digital age has redefined the boundaries of network marketing. Embracing technological tools, from social media platforms to AI-driven analytics, is no longer optional but vital.

169

3. Persistence: The Undying Flame

- **Understanding Persistence:** In the context of network marketing, persistence is not about mindlessly repeating actions but maintaining a resilient spirit in the face of challenges, rejections, and setbacks.

- **Persistence and Growth:** Each rejection is an opportunity for reflection and refinement. Instead of viewing challenges as roadblocks, they can be seen as stepping stones, shaping your journey and strengthening your resolve.

- **Harvesting the Fruits:** Persistence pays off over time. It may not be immediate, but consistent, genuine efforts, anchored in commitment and adaptability, yield long-term success.

Tab. 37: Persistence in Action

Challenge	Response
Rejection from Potential Clients	Seeking feedback, refining approach, understanding client needs better
Market Downturns	Diversifying product offerings, exploring new markets, upskilling
Technological Hurdles	Seeking training, collaborating with experts, staying updated on industry tech trends

In Summation

The roadmap to success in network marketing isn't a linear path laid with gold. It's a winding trail, with its peaks and valleys, storms and sunrises. Maxwell Bridge's vast experience elucidates that while techniques and trends are essential, the triumvirate of **Commitment, Adaptation, and Persistence** remains perennially relevant.

To quote Maxwell Bridge, *"In the world of network marketing, tools and tactics may shift, but the heart's core tenets remain unyielding. With Commitment, Adaptation, and Persistence as your compass, you don't merely navigate the storm; you become the master of your voyage."*

In your hands, dear reader, lies not just a book but a compass, guiding you through the myriad terrains of network marketing. Let these principles be your North Star, guiding you with unwavering precision toward the zenith of success.

Appendix

Further Reading and Resources

To navigate the world of network marketing, it's essential to rely on accurate, timely, and actionable resources. Beyond the insights shared by Maxwell Bridge, numerous authentic resources can further refine your approach to the industry. Here's a compilation of authoritative readings and platforms:

Books:

1. **"Go Pro: 7 Steps to Becoming a Network Marketing Professional"** by Eric Worre

   - A detailed manual that breaks down the key steps to becoming a successful network marketer.

2. **"Your First Year in Network Marketing: Overcome Your Fears, Experience Success, and Achieve Your Dreams!"** by Mark Yarnell and Rene Reid Yarnell

   - This book offers an honest look at the challenges and rewards of the first year in network marketing.

3. **"The Ultimate Guide to Network Marketing"** edited by Joe Rubino

- An anthology of advice from some of the most successful network marketers, providing varied perspectives and strategies.

4. **"Building an Empire: The Most Complete Blueprint to Building a Massive Network Marketing Business"** by Brian Carruthers

    - A guide that offers actionable strategies and insights for building a successful network marketing business.

Online Platforms and Journals:

1. **Direct Selling News** - A reputed online publication that provides articles on current trends, case studies, and interviews from the world of direct selling and network marketing. www.directsellingnews.com

2. **Networking Times** - This platform offers articles, tools, and resources to support network marketers in their growth journey. www.networkingtimes.com

3. **MLM.com** - A site that brings together experts from the industry to discuss various aspects of network marketing. www.mlm.com

Associations and Organizations:

1. **Direct Selling Association (DSA)** - A renowned organization that offers resources, research, and networking opportunities for

direct selling professionals. Their events and webinars are beneficial for anyone in the industry. www.dsa.org

2. **The Association of Network Marketing Professionals (ANMP)** - This organization focuses on the professional growth of its members, offering training sessions, conferences, and certifications for network marketers. www.anmp.com

Podcasts:

1. **"The Network Marketing Podcast"** hosted by Simon Chan

   - This podcast focuses on strategies, tips, and stories from top leaders in the network marketing industry.

2. **"The Robert Hollis Show"** hosted by Robert Hollis

   - Robert Hollis, a successful network marketer, shares insights, strategies, and motivational tips to help listeners succeed in the industry.

Concluding Note:

This list is a starting point for those looking to delve deeper into the world of network marketing. It is vital to continuously update your knowledge base, given the dynamic nature of the industry. Using the insights from Maxwell Bridge's guide in conjunction with these resources can serve as a solid foundation for success.

Tools and Platforms for Network Marketers

In our increasingly digitized age, tools and platforms play a pivotal role in reshaping and amplifying the strategies network marketers deploy. Harnessing the capabilities of contemporary technologies can empower professionals to reach wider audiences, maintain consistent engagement, and enhance operational efficiency. Maxwell Bridge, with his vast experience, undoubtedly understands the transformational potential of these digital assets. Here's a compilation of indispensable tools and platforms for both novice and veteran network marketers:

1. **Customer Relationship Management (CRM) Tools:**

   - **HubSpot**: An intuitive and powerful CRM tool, HubSpot allows network marketers to manage contacts, segment their audience, and schedule follow-ups, ensuring no potential lead is overlooked.

   - **Zoho CRM**: Tailored for businesses of all sizes, Zoho CRM facilitates real-time collaboration, lead management, and sales automation, enabling network marketers to foster meaningful relationships.

2. **Social Media Management and Analytics:**

- **Hootsuite**: This platform allows users to schedule posts, interact with followers, and get the analytics they need to improve social media strategies.

- **Buffer**: An easy-to-use platform that supports scheduling, publishing, and analyzing posts on multiple social media channels.

3. **Email Marketing Platforms:**

- **Mailchimp**: Beyond its primary function of email marketing, Mailchimp offers features like landing pages and customer segmentation, which can be particularly beneficial for network marketers.

- **ConvertKit**: Designed specifically for creators and small businesses, ConvertKit supports automated email campaigns and facilitates audience engagement.

4. **Digital Training and Webinar Platforms:**

- **Zoom**: An essential tool for virtual meetings and webinars. Its breakout room feature is particularly useful for network marketing team meetings or training sessions.

- **GoToWebinar**: A popular platform for hosting large-scale webinars, complete with analytics, audience interaction tools, and customizable branding.

5. **Affiliate and Referral Management:**

- **Post Affiliate Pro**: This platform assists businesses in managing their affiliate programs, ensuring transparency and efficiency in tracking referrals and commissions.

- **Ambassador**: A comprehensive referral marketing software that allows businesses to set up, track, and manage their referral marketing programs.

6. **Content Creation and Branding Tools:**

- **Canva**: With its user-friendly interface, Canva empowers network marketers to design anything from social media graphics to presentations, even without a design background.

- **Snappa**: A graphic design tool tailored for social media and marketing purposes. Its drag-and-drop editor ensures swift content creation.

7. **Project Management and Collaboration:**

- **Trello**: A visual tool that employs boards and cards to organize tasks, making project management straightforward and collaborative.

- **Slack**: Beyond being a messaging app, Slack is a collaboration hub that integrates with numerous other tools, ensuring seamless team communication.

Concluding Thoughts:

While the tools mentioned above have proven instrumental for numerous network marketers globally, it is paramount to remember that tools, in isolation, don't guarantee success. Their efficacy hinges on the strategic manner of their deployment. As Maxwell Bridge emphasizes, understanding the industry's nuances and integrating tools to enhance, not replace, human interactions is the key to true success in network marketing. As the adage goes, "It's not the wand but the wizard that makes the magic." Choose your tools wisely and use them strategically for optimal results.

Summary

183

186

188

189

Tables Index